the world in ONE SQUARE MILE

DO SOMETHING RADICAL IN TODAY'S GENERATION — TAKE INTEREST IN SOMEONE OTHER THAN YOURSELF.

Ten community-building ways love casts out the fear of others

Adam Bowles

WESTBOW
PRESS®
A DIVISION OF THOMAS NELSON
& ZONDERVAN

Copyright © 2017 Adam Bowles.

All rights reserved. No part of this book may be used or reproduced by any means, graphic, electronic, or mechanical, including photocopying, recording, taping or by any information storage retrieval system without the written permission of the author except in the case of brief quotations embodied in critical articles and reviews.

Scripture quotations marked (NIV) are taken from the Holy Bible, New International Version®, NIV®. Copyright © 1973, 1978, 1984, 2011 by Biblica, Inc.™ Used by permission of Zondervan. All rights reserved worldwide. www.zondervan.com The "NIV" and "New International Version" are trademarks registered in the United States Patent and Trademark Office by Biblica, Inc.™

Scripture quotations are taken from the Holy Bible, New Living Translation, copyright ©1996, 2004, 2007, 2013, 2015 by Tyndale House Foundation. Used by permission of Tyndale House Publishers, Inc., Carol Stream, Illinois 60188. All rights reserved.

WestBow Press books may be ordered through booksellers or by contacting:

WestBow Press
A Division of Thomas Nelson & Zondervan
1663 Liberty Drive
Bloomington, IN 47403
www.westbowpress.com
1 (866) 928-1240

Because of the dynamic nature of the Internet, any web addresses or links contained in this book may have changed since publication and may no longer be valid. The views expressed in this work are solely those of the author and do not necessarily reflect the views of the publisher, and the publisher hereby disclaims any responsibility for them.

ISBN: 978-1-5127-9399-4 (sc)
ISBN: 978-1-5127-9398-7 (hc)
ISBN: 978-1-5127-9400-7 (e)

Library of Congress Control Number: 2017910982

Print information available on the last page.

WestBow Press rev. date: 07/24/2017

One year. 120 stories. One square mile.

In what is part memoir, part call-to-action, Adam Bowles shares 10 community-building lessons he uncovered as he ventured out his front door and into his hometown of Jewett City, Conn., to do something radical in today's generation — take an interest in others. As division grows across the nation, it's time we listen again to the stories of our neighbors, and celebrate the threads of life that unite us all. These insights on faith, family and friendship, and views on race relations, immigration, the heroin crisis, the power of testimonies, what it means to be a hero and more, are woven into a narrative that can apply in one square miles nationwide.

Dedicated first to my Lord and Savior, Jesus Christ, and then my wife, Luisa, and my daughters, Tori and Roni. You fill my life with love and laughter.

ACKNOWLEDGEMENTS

A special thanks to my wife, Luisa, who went on drives with me as I searched for the next interview and who has been the one to listen the most to my hopes and dreams, sometimes in painstaking detail that could only be heard with much love and patience. For that matter, thank you to my daughters, Tori and Roni!

I want to acknowledge United Community and Family Services in Norwich for being the first to contribute to the online project and the production of this book.

Jono Wibberley, my brother-in-law, created the original logo for The World in One Square Mile, and has worked with me on various projects. The projects themselves were a success if only because of the fact that I was able to work with someone I appreciate so much.

Thank you to Greg Hartzell, who photographed many of the photos for the original project on Facebook, and who took interest in the initiative as we discussed it over several breakfasts.

And, finally, thank you to everyone who followed the stories online and who took the time to encourage me.

CONTENTS

Acknowledgements ix
Introduction xiii
The World Outside My Front Door 1
The World Found in the Ordinary 17
The World Shared in the Power of a Testimony 39
The World Found in Intergenerational Connections 52
The World Found in the Beauty of Many Races 66
The World Found among Our Immigrant Neighbors 84
The World of Big Stories in Small Towns 103
The World Found Through the Power of Observation 132
The World in One Square Mile 154
The World Waiting At Home 170

INTRODUCTION

After thirty years of living in the one square mile of Jewett City, I decided to fight any lingering negative perceptions of my hometown by spending a year interviewing 120 neighbors and visitors and posting the mostly spontaneous stories to Facebook.

I called the series The World in One Square Mile because the vignettes wove into a bigger picture, telling a greater story about the world we live in and about the need to break down walls among our neighbors as we have vulnerable, courageous conversations again.

Initially, I only intended to compile the stories into a photo book for my hometown.

But in the process of meeting people, I discovered a beautiful diversity and the untold stories of faith, family, and friendship in a way that I began to believe would inspire communities across the nation. I wanted others to take their own journeys out their front doors and into the world waiting to be found in their one square miles—wherever that may be and whenever people pass them by.

While the following is part-memoir—including my experience as a pastor and my background as a journalist—it is more importantly a national call to action. The project suddenly felt timely—urgent even. *In one of the most narcissistic generations of all time, this is a call to take interest in, listen to, and demonstrate empathy for others. In a time of great division, this is a call to focus on what unites us, the common threads to all of our stories.*

While the profiles I wrote may have only scratched the surface of people's lives—catching them in a moment on the sidewalk or in a parking lot or at the park—collectively they cut deep into our identity not only as local residents, but as Americans. If 2016 was the year of division, we now need to return to unity. We need to *listen* to one another again. President Barrack Obama shared this timely advice in his farewell address: "If you're tired of arguing with strangers on the Internet, try talking to one of them in real life."

It's gotten to the point where the University of Connecticut launched a three-year, $5.75 million project called Humility and Conviction in Public Life to investigate how intellectual humility can promote healthier and more meaningful public conversation, according to Michael Lynch, professor of philosophy and director of the Humanities Institute. In the spring 2017 edition of *UConn Magazine*, Mr. Lynch described intellectual humility as "being aware of our own cognitive limitations and biases, and being responsive to the evidence." This project doesn't specifically focus on public discourse but does advocate for a practical humility that actually demonstrates interest in others by inquiring about their stories and shuns the prevailing "selfie" attitude that says I am the most interesting person in the room and people should only care about what I have to say.

Rick Warren, author of the *Purpose Driven Life*, put it this way: "You see pain with your eyes, but you sympathize with your ears. Sometimes the greatest way to serve someone is just by listening."

The stories that follow demonstrate ten community-building ways love casts out the fear of others as well as questions for discussion and other specific suggestions for next steps. The insights will help develop empathy, teach the power of personal stories, demonstrate the need to listen to one another, and expand your vision of the world all to make deeper connections among neighbors. They also include insights on faith, race relations, immigration, the heroin crisis, the values of small town life and more. I trust this will benefit neighbors nationwide, but also inspire practical applications for church volunteers, educators, community leaders, town officials and others.

The interviews for Facebook were mostly with strangers, some as they passed by my sidewalk. When was the last time you cried? What was a challenge in your life you had to overcome? I asked these and other life questions and the answers showed no one is ordinary—everyone has an amazing story to share. For anyone of us, a cup of coffee, a brief yet meaningful conversation with a stranger, and walls will come down, one square mile at a time.

I didn't want to hype the borough. But I also didn't want to feed a negative reputation by leading people with questions about drugs and crime and poverty. I wanted people to tell their stories in their words. In effect, they came up with the project's themes.

I sought a variety of voices—male and female, old and young, black and white. I gained a greater appreciation of those I knew well once I dug a little deeper into their stories. That was another lesson in itself. The interviews were often relatively short—a half hour or so. Of the 120 profiles, about half of the stories are woven into this narrative and were selected because they spoke to the larger themes. Many of the profiles appear more or less the same as the Facebook posts, although now with context and personal commentary. For the ones I was able to get permission, I used the names of the people I met. For the others, I left their names out to protect their privacy.

It will also help you to know that the window in which I view the world is one as a follower of Jesus. People love to quote famous people and experts in stories like this. I love to quote the Bible, which I do several times in the following pages. I am compelled by the love of God and the value of every soul made in His image. I think of the scripture in Jeremiah 29:7 (NIV) that says, "Seek the peace and prosperity of the city to which I have carried you into exile. Pray to the LORD for it, because if it prospers, you too will prosper." I want the communities we live in here in the United States to prosper, and to do that we must cast out fear of others through His love.

That is why you will see some of the following stories tied to something simple that my wife and I do each week, along with other families in the church where I serve as one of the pastors. We host what we call cell groups, or gatherings in our living rooms, where we share messages of hope from the Bible and Christian testimonies. We call them cell groups because, like cells in a body, we pray they ultimately multiply. Several people I interviewed and met for the very first time ended up becoming guests in our home for these meetings. That was my personal practical application of the lessons I learned through this initiative.

So this is partly my story as a neighbor, writer, and one of the pastors of a nearby church in Norwich. I love adventure. I love visiting faraway places. I love assignments that have taken me to faraway peoples. But this is the story of a journey out my front door and into my hometown. I've always wanted to travel the world, but I found the world in one square mile. And I found just how much God is at work in the lives of ordinary people.

It can be easy for visionaries and dreamers to forget about starting their journeys with where they are. It's interesting to me that some scholars say the walled city of Jerusalem was less than one square mile when Jesus ministered and when the disciples first stood united with a gospel message that would change the world forever. My question to you is: what would happen if we stood united with that same spirit in our one square miles?

Why the One Square Mile of Jewett City?

As a sixth-grader in Lisbon, Connecticut, I wasn't exactly tuned in to the greater complexities and interconnectedness of the world around me in 1986. I loved baseball, girls, and G.I. Joe. (Although, with the latter I was highly embarrassed when my best friend and I exchanged action figures in the hallway on what was supposed to be a secret mission, but turned into a preteen nightmare as they spilled out from my locker onto the floor in front of the passing aforementioned girls.) Still, I was learning at this tender age that somehow the things that do happen in this world can suddenly hurdle into the cradle of my heart and rock it mercilessly. That year, Christa McAuliffe, a teacher from Concord, New Hampshire, was one of seven crew members to be killed during the mission of the Space Shuttle Challenger. The news strangely unsettled me. A year earlier, my parents had divorced. That continued to unsettle me the most.

The divorce triggered a series of local moves for me, my mother, and my sister. I cried when I learned we were permanently leaving our home in Preston, where my backyard was a boy's paradise of nearly two hundred acres of adventures marked by secret forts I built out of sticks. I loved to put my treasures—a toy, a rock, a feather, among other items—in a McDonald's Happy Meal cardboard box, hook the handles to a stick, and trek to a place I called the Mossy Spot with my younger sister, Sara, and our Golden Retriever Daisy by my side. This was my favorite place in the whole world—a carpet of moss spread out under several trees that I was convinced I had alone discovered by ducking through a clearing near a trail. I would lie down in the moss and stare into the clouds, daydreaming about who knows what. Probably baseball. Maybe my next fort. But not Lisbon. And definitely not Jewett City. After a year in Lisbon, I had finally settled. I loved my friends, my baseball and basketball teams, and looked forward to the next school year. But then my mom called me and my sister into her bedroom and broke the news. The family we were living with was moving, and so we would be moving too, starting over in the adjoining town. The tears spilled down my face again. "Jewett City?" I said in between sobs. "But that's where all the criminals live!"

I don't know exactly why I made that association. Although, a serial killer named Michael Ross was on the prowl in Eastern Connecticut. He was an insurance agent who lived in Jewett City. When police searched for a body near our property in Preston, my mom's sense of security deep in the woods suddenly evaporated, and we hurriedly packed some belongings and rushed out of the house to stay with friends. Okay, so that is a strong reason for the association. Still, I don't even know if I realized then that he was from the borough. Mom reassured me everything would be fine. But when we moved in with friends on Elm Street, the first kid on the block I met walked me down to a path at the bottom of the road and, once we got off the street, asked, "Want to see my knife?" He pulled out a switchblade. I gulped. Jewett City has been my home ever since—a thirty-one-year relationship.

During this time, the borough struggled with an image problem. In 1997, two years into my career as a journalist at the *Norwich Bulletin*, the local newspaper nine miles away from my home, a colleague penned a column with the headline, "Burg on map for all the wrong reasons." (Jewett City is the borough of the town of Griswold.) He cited three acts of violence and an arson and wrote, "It's not fair to cast a sweeping blame for an entire town. There are many good people there. You would like to think most of them are. But the tidbits above are only the highlights from one month in Jewett City. Stories like these seem to keep coming out of this town at an alarming rate. This tiny burg of about 3,000 people seems to have more troubles and troublemakers than a town 10 times its size. When was the last time you heard of rampant crime in nearby towns like Voluntown, Canterbury, Lisbon?" Well, my answer twenty years later is those towns don't have a downtown, as much poverty, or as high a population density. In 2015, a silly, gimmicky survey named Jewett City as the most redneck town in the state. I shrugged it off at first. I certainly wouldn't describe it like that. After all, I live here! But then I wanted to push back on yet another skewed perception, yet another stereotype.

It also reignited an idea to write about life in my hometown that I had been carrying around in my head and in scribbled notes for seven years. When I drove by a banner outside of Altone's Restaurant on Main Street that celebrated the borough's 120th anniversary, *it* suddenly crystalized. Right then and there I knew I needed to write 120 profiles of people who live in, work in, or visit the borough. I prayed that night about whether to take that step. I suppose it was the fear of failure in the town I lived in that made me hesitate even after all those years.

And now, a project birthed in one of the poorest communities in New England is drawing national, albeit modest, attention and is the subject of an equity and social justice initiative.

 I thought I knew Jewett City because I grew up here, lived here all my adult life, and was even assigned to cover the town as part of my first beat at the *Bulletin* just months after graduating from the University of Connecticut in 1995. But it was more of an acquaintance until I stopped and began talking to people outside of my friends circle.

 I had almost no idea who I'd come across for this project. Or the lessons I'd learn. The important thing was that I start—start with that first hello, that first interview, that first post. And start here at home, in a borough with a population now of about 3,500 people. I started with a woman I met at the Griswold Veterans Memorial Park as she sat on a wooden fence. She was reticent at first, but once she got going it was hard to stop her! The New York transplant described herself: "I'm not the huggy type. I'm not the smooshy type. I'm hello-how-are-you-doing type and then I go." Her story elicited the first reader response on Facebook: *"My lovely neighbor!!!!"* It was short and sweet but encouraged me tremendously. I realized right away this would be an opportunity to celebrate and get to know our neighbors. Readers' comments would prove to be a dynamic part of this project. Many are included in the pages to follow, even if not with their names, and are without alteration from their original posts with the stories. In fact, I saw the positive power of social media, and specifically Facebook—the platform I used to reach a local audience. The woman from the park still waves at me when I drive by in my green 2002 Toyota Tundra.

 It was stories like this that prompted my dear friend, Jen Hardy, to write an encouragement to the Facebook page very early in the series: "I have sat here with tears running down my face reading these beautiful stories about real people—real lives. Please keep sharing them, thank you for the people who are willing to share a part of themselves. What a beautiful Square Mile xxx" I agree—it is a beautiful square mile. In fact, due to the search for what makes this borough shine, and for the prayers that have gone along with that search, and for the people precious in God's sight that I found here, you could call it Jewel City.

I also spent most of the time on this project carrying a secret that only my wife and a few friends knew. Eventually, I shared the news with my two daughters. And that secret was, as I was getting to know my hometown on a deeper level, and as strangers were becoming friends, I was preparing to move overseas to support a Christian musical my sister had written called *Heaven on Earth*. Just like when I was a boy moving from Preston to Lisbon and then Lisbon to Jewett City, the girls cried. As I drove down side streets, stopped by the parks, or coasted along main street, observing faces, getting the pulse of the town through its ebbs and flows, I had my own times of tears as I thought of the pain of saying goodbye to all that is familiar and the people I love, believing the will of God is the safest, best home to live in. So, in part, this is also my hello and goodbye. Or more like so long for now.

THE WORLD OUTSIDE MY FRONT DOOR

Lesson #1: Be the One to Start the Conversation and Start with Where You Are

At the time of this writing, I live in a Victorian home with peeling, white paint and gray trim and a front porch secluded by a row of bushes and three large maple trees on the edge of the sidewalk. Our home on East Main Street is directly across the Second Congregational Church. Our street intersects with a short side road called Hawkins Street that runs straight into A. A. Young Jr. Hose & Ladder Co., the borough's fire department. The back of the fire department abuts the Jewett City Little League complex, one of the most popular places in town in spring and summer. Jewett City itself is the borough of the town of Griswold, where two of the world's largest casinos are less than a half-hour drive away, and yet where the town's biggest attraction is an ice-cream stand at a farm made regionally famous due to its highly photographed sunflower field.

I moved into my home when I was a junior in high school. One of our pastors, a man who I looked up to as my closest mentor in life, invited me and my mom and sister to live with his family on the spacious third floor of the house to help ease the financial burden on my mother. I would be trading the entire third floor of the house we lived in on Ashland Street, which was effectively my teenage bachelor's pad, for a tiny third floor room in the new house. But, unlike my previous moves, I jumped at the opportunity. After about six years, I moved out when Luisa and I got married in 1995. We moved to an apartment also in the borough and then to a house on Faust Street that had been foreclosed, whose backyard connected to the house I returned to. When my pastor friend put his house on the market, I privately prayed that someone in our church would buy it. There were so many memories in this home that involved the church—picnics, youth groups, prayer meetings, hosting of overseas guests. I watched as the price of the home slid along with the housing market. One day I suddenly realized it had slid far enough that I could possibly buy it! We made the leap, and it has been our home for the last nine years, where we have created our own memories with picnics, youth groups, dinners with friends, campfires, prayer meetings, and more.

My study is on the second floor, where a cushioned window seat overlooks the street. My desk looks like it was custom-made for the room. But the truth is I eyed the piece of furniture at a local store, decided it would be perfect for my needs, and purchased it without ever measuring it or my wall. When it was delivered, the two workers expressed skepticism that it would actually fit. It did, but only after they cut away the floor trim to give an extra inch on either side of the wall. In my literary mind, I have always considered the desk a symbol of how guided spontaneity is sometimes better than waiting until everything measures up.

It's from this study window that I came across several of the people I would profile. I'd spot someone or a couple of people walking along the sidewalk by my front door or along the sidewalk across the street, and I'd rush outside to meet them and ask if they'd mind if I interviewed them for a short story. Most of them said yes. Sometimes I put my sneakers by the front door instead of the back door where we enter our house to save time. Once I didn't have time to even put on my sneakers. In the middle of the interview with Alisha Martin, her niece, Madison, looked down at my feet and laughed. "You're just in your socks," she said. Alisha has become a friend of the family, so at least I didn't scare them off.

The idea was simple, if not convenient for me. Who are the people who walk by my front door every day? What are their stories? What makes them special? It seems like we either don't think about these questions enough or don't have the courage to actually approach people. Asking people questions about their lives, instead of talking about our own, is a form of selflessness. And when people begin to talk, their hearts unfold along with their dreams, their hopes, and their sorrows. If only we would ask! I found one of my favorite all-time quotes in a textbook—*Writing and Reporting for the Media*—I used for a journalism class I taught at Three Rivers Community College in Norwich. "Language most shows a man; speak that I may see thee," said Ben Jonson, English poet and playwright.

One of the people I met for this project posted on Facebook about a word used to describe this feeling in more specific terms—*sonder*. It's in the Urban Dictionary, so it's not official, but I still like it. It's "the realization that each random passerby is living a life as vivid and complex as your own—populated with their own ambitions, friends, routines, worries and inherited craziness—an epic story that continues invisibly around you like an anthill sprawling deep underground, with elaborate passageways to thousands of other lives that you'll never know existed, in which you might appear only once, as an extra sipping coffee in the background, as a blur of traffic passing on the highway, as a lighted window at dusk." (Ironic that I later interviewed her as she randomly passed by one day along Main Street.)

In New England, especially, it's not exactly customary to approach strangers and strike up a conversation. It's not the social norm to pause and get to know the people who surround us. It's not like it never happens here in the borough. Hey, if you take your dog for a walk, then it seems you have the easiest chance to interact with neighbors. But these approaches with people we don't know are not common. Everybody is so busy. We are all in such a rush to get to our next destination. We tend to judge people on appearances without even taking the time to get to know their full stories. And in New England, where stone walls mark territories that no longer need marking, people erect invisible walls of fear and mistrust that maintain various degrees of separation.

I enjoy chatting with strangers from time to time. But I also have to overcome feeling self-conscious and the part of me that just wants to get to where I'm going or be left to my own thoughts. As a teenager at a church overseas I was visiting for a few weeks, the mother in the family where I was staying challenged me one day. "Why do you just stand in the corner?" she asked me of my routine when the service ended. "You need to go out of your way to talk to people." I was embarrassed by her bluntness. I wanted to make excuses. But she was right, so I pushed myself to interact with others at the church, whether they took the initiative or not. I surprised myself in the process. I really enjoyed getting to know people even if I felt awkward and shy at times.

This project, of course, made it easy to talk to people. It was my excuse. And I'm so grateful for it. It also convinced me of something—we suffer from an epidemic of silence. Sometimes, we silence ourselves. Sometimes, we are silenced by others. But behind the veil of silence is the face of that which makes life beautiful.

The first person I approached outside my home—and just the second story of the series—was a twenty-seven-year-old man who lived in nearby Norwich. From my study window, I saw a stuffed toy cat peeking out of a backpack he was carrying and it stirred my curiosity. It was an October afternoon and small piles of brown leaves had collected along the sidewalk. "This is for my son," he told me after I introduced myself. We were standing at the corner of East Main Street and Hawkins Street, just yards away from the congregational church. "I want to finally be good enough for him. I want to be strong enough for him. My father left me when I was one year old. He just sold everything in the house and left. I'm going to vow to do better for my children, for my son." The man was in Jewett City to stay a night at a friend's house. He said his son was temporarily in foster care while he, the father, completed drug and alcohol counseling.

I had conducted interviews for fifteen years at the newspaper, and even taught students in that introductory journalism class at Three Rivers how to conduct interviews. But I still didn't quite know how to conduct the ones I was going to do for One Square Mile. I had written profiles for the *Norwich Bulletin*, but those were typically of people referred to us. I had done on-the-street interviews for the newspaper, but those were with specific topics in mind. I was also influenced by the work of Brandon Stanton, who is famous for his photographs and accompanying quotes for a Facebook project called "Humans of New York," which has more than 18 million likes. I tried his style with the first person I interviewed, but it didn't quite work for me. For one thing, Brandon is a professional photographer. I just use my iPhone for most of the pictures—it's a form of backpack journalism. And I'm also used to a more traditional story format.

In any case, this interview was short but immediately left a powerful impact on me. He said so much about his life in such few words. And to me, a stranger! He was a father abandoned by his own father—a much too common theme for young men in this area. He had a story of drugs and alcohol and family, and all of this was clearly on his mind as he was walking by just twenty feet from my home. He was a man with a vow, and our conversation forced me to reflect on that. Indeed, he was solemn about his mission. A mission to do better. Vows are supposed to make families and communities stronger. At weddings, we say until death do us part. But the reality is that more and more Americans are suffering from broken promises, vows unfulfilled. Politicians. Married couples. Parents. Church-goers. We need to renew our vows, join the mission—God's mission—to do better for the sake of our children.

I saw him once or twice more walking through town, but haven't noticed him since. I'm left though with the memory of that stuffed animal and what it represented—the hope of a father to give his son the chance he never had.

I got three responses from readers directed to the man I wrote about:

You can do it.

Good luck; you'll need it.

And then from a former *Bulletin* colleague, Kate Carey-Trull: *Touching. Hope he follows through, it will be challenging.*

Later that month, I stopped Josaphat Yvan-Harold and his son, Jonathan, fifteen, as they were walking by my house. I invited them inside my home on the spot, and they agreed. I had worried people would consider me an intrusion. Some indeed denied my requests to interview them, but it ultimately proved to be a needless worry. Far more people agreed to talk.

We sat around my dining room table. My wife came downstairs surprised to see our guests. I had interrupted their walk back from a pharmacy downtown and to their home on Monroe Avenue just outside the borough, but still in Griswold.

The father and son shared that they endure a painful separation several months of the year. Josaphat lives in Port-au-Prince, Haiti.

Their Haitian roots immediately captivated me. Conversations inevitably lead to connections, as in this case. From the moment I first reported on the stories of the Haitian community in neighboring Norwich, I fell in love with the people. I attended their boisterous Haitian flag days, grieved with friends at funerals of Haitian family members, and celebrated and danced at weddings of Haitian friends.

I visited Haiti in 2010, one month after an earthquake killed about 300,000 people and left 1.3 million people homeless. I still remember the aftershocks that struck fear in our missionary group, which included me and members of the First Haitian Baptist Church of Norwich and a French mailman who worked in the neighborhood of the church. The last aftershock on the night before we left unsettled us so much that the five of us took our pillows and blankets and slept outside on the cold, hard steps to the villa where we were staying.

Jonathan, along with his mother and his seventeen-year-old sister, Thara, had lived in Griswold for nearly eight years, moving here from Norwich. Jonathan was just four months old when he moved with his family to the United States because life was dangerous in Haiti and his grandmother was a resident of Miami who was able to sponsor them. Eventually, Josaphat set up a job for his wife at nearby Mohegan Sun casino.

Josaphat was working as an agronomist and a professor and had traveled to several countries. He could speak German, Spanish, English, Creole, French, and Latin.

Jonathan told me it can be challenging to be in a family with two dominant cultures. "But most of the time it's kind of cool, especially with my friends because they don't know about my culture," he said. "I can teach them that. Like my sister's friends want to know about Haitian cuisine." His attitude of having feet in two worlds was so refreshingly positive compared to the often acrimonious national discourse about immigration.

Of all his world travels, Josaphat told me he particularly enjoyed his time in Germany from 1965–67. "It was twenty years after the Second World War. I found all the people were very young. We passed the time talking about war. The German people (shared) how war is not good." Josaphat had a government job in Haiti during the regimes of two dictators—Francois "Papa Doc" Duvalier and Jean Claude "Baby Doc" Duvalier. "Anybody could die on any day," Josaphat said. In one particularly dangerous assignment, Josaphat was told to collect debt from an army general who had refused to pay the bank his loan. The first several meetings were tense but eventually they became "good friends."

At the time I spoke with him, Josaphat had been here for one month and planned to return to Haiti in a few weeks. He planned to return to Griswold in April and to stay for a few months to see his daughter graduate from Griswold High School. Jonathan told me he enjoyed cross-country and concert choir and looked forward to working with the sound crew for the spring musical. My daughter, Victoria, was in the musical, *Jesus Christ Superstar*, so when we saw each other again we exchanged fist bumps. And I saw them at Thara's graduation. I attended the ceremony because Tori was also graduating. As we stepped out of the school and into the courtyard on this highly emotional day, one of the largest groups of all the families posed together for photos. I recognized the Haitian father and son in that gathering.

We continue to acknowledge each other on the street or at school events. It's a nice feeling. One of those events was the high school's winter concert. My daughter, Veronica, a freshman at the time, was in the choir. In the center of dozens of choir members was Jonathan, seemingly the most animated of all the students as he smiled and swayed with the music. I connected with his performance because I knew his story. He stood out in the crowd. A name attached to a face. A student with a dream.

Readers' responses:
What a wonderful story of a Beautiful family! God bless your family! Amazing

One day in April, I had the pleasure of talking with Ida Rounseville, who was with her two granddaughters and who I stopped just outside the entrance of my driveway. I had never noticed her before. She described her eleven-year-old granddaughter, Angel, as a "miracle baby." Naturally, that got my attention, and I asked her more about that particular part of the story. After Angel was born she underwent three open-heart surgeries to correct a heart defect. But now Angel is healthy and happy, Ida said. Angel agreed: "I like to sing, dance, play football, baseball, basketball, archery—all sports." I loved her youthful zeal for life.

I felt blessed to hear a story about a walking miracle—one that walked right by my house. I would soon learn there are lots of walking miracles in Jewett City. That encouraged my faith. Miracles fill the Gospels. Jesus raised the dead, caused the blind to see, walked on water, and multiplied a few fishes and loaves to feed thousands. In these cases, the only possible explanation was divine intervention. We overuse the word *miracle* now, often applying it to situations where perhaps natural factors contributed to the amazing results. Still, miracles not only fill the Gospels, they fill our streets. God is always at work, even if we aren't always looking. It's a matter of what we allow ourselves to see. Even many of those who saw Jesus do miracles still didn't believe, still didn't give God the proper credit. I like the way Ida applied the word *miracle* here because Angel was near death and is now alive and well. If we pay attention, we will see the fingerprints of God in the everyday happenings of creation.

Ida took Angel and her seven-year-old sister, Brandy Ray, for a walk that Friday afternoon from her home on Tift Street to Jewett City Pizza Palace for grinders. The girls' mother, Nicole Johnson, was living on the Mashantucket Indian reservation in Ledyard. "I have them on weekends and whenever I can get them," Ida said of her only two grandchildren.

Ida had moved here from South Kingston, Rhode Island, three years ago after landing a supply job at Two Trees Inn at Foxwoods Resort Casino, one of the largest casinos in the world. She is a member of the Mashantucket Pequot tribe and is from the Narragansett tribe of Rhode Island. Her American Indian roots is an active part of her family's tapestry; they attend powwows and pass on stories of their past. "Like the war," Brandy interjected, referring to the 1637 Pequot War, when the Connecticut and Massachusetts colonies attacked a Mystic fort, killing approximately 600 Pequots.

Angel and Brandy said they loved spending time with their grandmother. "She's funny," Brandy said. "She's strong for...never mind," Angel added, glancing sideways at Ida. Brandy finished her sentence: "for the elderly." They all laughed.

I left that twenty-minute interview reflecting on something I found fascinating. Tucked away in this tiny borough was not only a walking miracle, but a walking history lesson waiting to be told. Actually, it was being told in the way stories have always been shared—via oral tradition. An event that stretched back 380 years was still part of the psyche of one of my neighbors in a way that I could not directly relate, but certainly could learn from. What if she shared her story with more than just her family, but also with her neighbors and with her community? Would her heritage become part of our collective heritage and allow us in one small way to address any walls that may exist between the Mashantucket tribe and the surrounding communities, for example? Books, museums, and media help connect us to our past. But this is also how history comes alive.

Readers' responses:
God must have bigger plans for her.

Then there were two passing teenagers I stopped and talked with. Throughout the year, I saw once again how important it is for the voices of teenagers to be raised in our communities. They desperately want to be heard, to be considered, to know their opinions count. And their stories captivated me, even if we just scratched the surface.

I interviewed a fourteen-year-old girl who had just planned a celebration for her boyfriend's fifteenth birthday the previous Sunday, but for three hours he went missing. She cried. Finally, she got a text from him. The boyfriend said he had gotten lost outdoors and ended up walking the railroad tracks that cut through town for three hours. In a way, the incident touched on one of the girlfriend's biggest fears—abandonment. "My family kind of had issues when I was younger so I'm always afraid people are going to leave me," the girlfriend said. She was living with her mother in the borough at the time.

The couple was headed to a nearby street, where the boyfriend was living with his mother, to watch movies and celebrate his birthday a day late. He has two older sisters. His dad was living in Taftville. The girlfriend carried an inhaler for her asthma. A punk rock song by All Time Low played from her cell phone speaker. The girlfriend, who had five older sisters and one older brother living in various places in Connecticut, moved to Jewett City from Putnam nine years ago. She said it was the best thing that ever happened to her because of all the friends she has made here.

The pain of abandonment bubbled up as a common denominator among people I interviewed. I needed to first listen before I could then see that need with greater sensitivity. I could relate to family strains through my experience as a child, but God healed me. God has promised me He will never leave me, nor forsake me. It's a promise I've shared with others so many times. But here I was face-to-face with the bruising, cold reality that has swept so much of this teenage girl's generation. No wonder she cried as her boyfriend wandered the tracks. My wife and I happened to drive by her months later as she and a few friends walked the neighborhood on Halloween night. I pray that teens who feel abandoned will be heard, healed, and helped in the communities they live in. Sometimes, we make the mistake to think this work needs to be done primarily through massive organizational activities. But personal connections with trustworthy families and mentors who share their lives with them often prove to be more effective. It doesn't cost money to lend a listening ear; it's one of the most powerful, loving acts we can show someone.

Across the street from my house I occasionally glanced out my window and noticed two men renovating the front of the Second Congregational Church during a stretch of a few weeks. Eventually, I crossed the street to learn that Cody Pearson thinks every day about his dad, Andy, who died of a heart attack when Cody was a sophomore at Griswold High School.

Cody's mother, Susan, was a bus driver in town. Cody, nineteen, and a 2015 Griswold High School graduate, has five brothers and two sisters.

"He was quiet," Cody said of his father, Andy. "But we understood each other."

For the last couple of weeks, Cody had been working with Chris Kempesta, fifty-nine, of JXN Renovations to build a handicapped ramp and stairs at the church. Cody landed a job with Chris a year earlier when one of Cody's high school teachers referred him to Chris.

Chris named the business after his son, Jackson, thirteen. Chris has another son, Christopher, thirty-six, from a previous marriage who was living in Oklahoma. Chris began his business ten years ago after being laid off as a splicing supervisor for what was then SNET. The company had offered him a job in New Haven, but he declined.

"There's two to three shootings a day," Chris said, recalling his reaction. "I don't want to be one of them. If I'm going to be in the news, I want it to be for doing some good for someone."

A friend in Mystic who he hadn't heard from in a year called him to say he had heard Chris had lost his job. He gave him some work to do and talked about the challenges of self-employment, which included saying goodbye to the six weeks of vacation Chris had earned while in the corporate world.

Chris had been married to Kelly, a physical therapist, for twenty years at that time. During their marriage, he didn't want to have children because he enjoyed his comfortable lifestyle. He and Kelly would often sit on their back porch, drink a couple of cocktails, and make impulse decisions to travel to such places as Florida, where his brothers live, with as little as a week's notice. When Kelly became unexpectedly pregnant, Chris went through a difficult adjustment. "But now that he's here, he's a good kid. He's smart. He's on the honor society." Chris has supported Jackson through his years of playing baseball at Jewett City Little League, where Chris was serving as the treasurer.

Chris had lived off Route 201 in Griswold since 1991, drawn here from nearby Taftville thanks to an inexpensive, new house that offered nearly three acres to enjoy. While working on the job at the church, a couple nearby regularly stopped by to chat about the progress. Chris and Kelly are also close friends with Mary Lou Morrissette, who lives across the street from the church and next door to me. Someone from a church in Sterling drove by and stopped to ask if Chris could do a similar job at his church. Word-of-mouth was the primary way he would get work. That's how it is for small town life here.

"I like my job," Chris said. "But it's like any job. Some days are better than others."

All told, I spoke with twenty-five people I met for the first time more or less right outside my front door. I learned it's important to cross the road and begin the conversation. In fact, by not reaching out we miss out on so much. We need to lift the veil of silence. You never know what you will learn. You never know the friend you might make. You never know how much one word of encouragement can lift the spirits of a neighbor.

In a way, this is at the heart of the famous biblical story of the Good Samaritan, found here in Luke 10:25–37 (NIV). Keep in mind, Jews and Samaritans hated each other. Socially, they were taught to avoid one another. Jesus was asked: "Who is my neighbor?" In reply Jesus said:

> A man was going down from Jerusalem to Jericho, when he was attacked by robbers. They stripped him of his clothes, beat him and went away, leaving him half dead. A priest happened to be going down the same road, and when he saw the man, he passed by on the other side. So too, a Levite, when he came to the place and saw him, passed by on the other side. But a Samaritan, as he traveled, came where the man was; and when he saw him, he took pity on him. He went to him and bandaged his wounds, pouring on oil and wine. Then he put the man on his own donkey, brought him to an inn and took care of him. The next day he took out two denarii and gave them to the innkeeper. "Look after him," he said, "and when I return, I will reimburse you for any extra expense you may have."
>
> "Which of these three do you think was a neighbor to the man who fell into the hands of robbers?"
>
> The expert in the law replied, "The one who had mercy on him."
>
> Jesus told him, "Go and do likewise."

Indeed, let's go and do likewise. Stop avoiding others out of fear. Instead, reach out and bring help to them, even when—especially when—they are racially, ethnically or socioeconomically different from you. Some people are afraid not only to venture out of their hometowns and wherever they are most comfortable, but also to venture into their hometowns.

Think of the humanity that passed by my house this past year and passes by my house every day. The teenage girl lived with the fear of abandonment. Ida still spoke of the trauma of the 1637 Pequot War, whose history was the subject of an exhibit at the nearby Mashantucket Pequot Museum and Research Center. Jonathan's father still went back and forth to Haiti and learned from Germans about the horrors of war. The streets may be mostly quiet outside my front door, but the heart of each person explodes with life.

Action Steps and Reflection:

1. How can you start a conversation too? There's no way around it, you have to be bold. As long as boldness doesn't mean rudeness, you will actually make people more secure by showing your definite, sincere interest in them. I went from a shy approach to the blunt approach of, "Hi, can I do a story on you?" Many people would respond saying, "Who, me?" And then quickly follow with, "Sure." How easy or difficult do you think this would be for you?
2. Individuals: Reach out to the people in your immediate proximity. Smile at them. Wave. And talk! Determine to say hello and start a conversation. You just may start to see your neighborhood warm up and walls torn down. At your discretion, invite someone in for a cup of coffee. Or a meal. Write his or her story, or a snippet of his or her story, and, with permission, share on Facebook using #onesquaremile.
3. Churches: Jesus discerned the story of the woman at the well. He asked questions. He found common ground. We

focus so much on our own stories that we forget to hear the stories of others. Arrange an afternoon of training on how to write a brief profile. Start a Facebook series on your neighbors, featuring a photo of a church member with a neighbor or someone they randomly meet.

4. Communities: Ultimately, not everyone is going to start the conversation. We need trained community messengers, not just reporters at newspapers. Start a Facebook page or a blog. Train someone or a few people to interview others. High school students, college students, retired residents, and others would be willing to pick up their pens.

Josaphat Yvan-Harold, right, and his son, Jonathan

Ida Rounseville and her two granddaughters (photo by Greg Hartzell)

Cody Pearson, left, and Chris Kempesta

THE WORLD FOUND IN THE ORDINARY

Lesson #2: Celebrate the Local, Everyday Heroes That Are All around Us

I love finding the extraordinary in the ordinary. And with people, considering there are no two individuals created exactly alike, there is always plenty to find. No one is actually ordinary, except by false human standards of comparison that evaluates others through the lens of fame and fortune. Yes, some obviously have more influence than others. But that doesn't give those influencers more human value than others with less influence.

When I went to Honduras to write stories about the recovery from Hurricane Mitch in 1998, I had the opportunity to interview their president. I was excited about this once-in-a-lifetime chance until a friend relayed a message to me through my mother in a phone call. In so many words, she said, "What's the big deal?"

I was grateful for the blunt feedback because I would have been detoured from my original mission—write about the stories of everyday Hondurans who were suffering after the disaster. Of course, the interview could have been valuable in other ways. But in this case, with such a tight schedule, it wasn't worth an entire day of getting clearance all for a half-hour interview just because I found it impressive. Everyone had already heard from the president. Other voices needed to be raised. I stuck to the game plan and had the privilege to see firsthand how so-called ordinary people were overcoming massive obstacles in heroic ways that we could relate to back home in Connecticut. Like not just the stories of what the hurricane destroyed, but what the hurricane *could have* destroyed.

That included the lives of eleven babies who were cared for in an orphanage—the same orphanage my wife was adopted from—and were spared injury or worse despite a river fifty feet away from where they slept that turned into a raging torrent of trees and boulders that had been swept up from the mountainside.

The one square mile of Jewett City is as ordinary as a community gets. Traffic downtown—where there are two banks, two pharmacies, a post office, a library, a hardware store, town hall, a few restaurants, and a few other businesses—gets busy at certain times but mostly because drivers are passing through. I can't think of anything famous about it other than the fact that my father-in-law likes to point out we are the only community in the world that bears the name Jewett City. I don't know how to verify that exactly, but I suppose that's true.

We used to celebrate George Washington's visit to the borough. Until, as a reporter, I, with the help of the town historian, debunked that story as legend and rumor. Roger Lafrancois is from Jewett City. He played eight games as a back-up catcher for the Boston Red Sox in 1982 and spent years as a minor league baseball hitting coach. He's a local sports hero, even if his life is defined as more than just that. Still, in terms of fame, that's about the peak of it all for this borough.

The American obsession with fame is quite a destructive force. Most people wouldn't say anyone is unimportant, and yet our actions show we believe exactly that. It's antithetical to our Declaration of Independence, which reads: "We hold these truths to be self-evident, that all men are created equal, that they are endowed by their Creator with certain unalienable Rights, that among these are Life, Liberty and the pursuit of Happiness."

It is self-evident. Our Creator has endowed each one of us for life, liberty, and happiness. And yet it's easy to overlook these common passions and pursuits in the people we become too familiar with in our lives.

It would be easy to overlook Mick Gardner, for instance. I've known Mick for years. Or, I should say, I've known *of* Mick for years. I bumped into him often at Anthony's Hardware Store on Main Street, where he worked for thirteen years. He knew where nearly every nut and bolt was in that store and would lead me down narrow, crowded aisles crammed with all types of home improvement items to find whatever I needed. His brother, Scott, was a friend of mine when I was in high school and then college. So when I spotted Mick walking by my house, I invited him inside for the first time. He seemed uncomfortable, and it was a difficult interview in the sense that he didn't have much to say and the questions quickly led to dead-ends, no matter how open-ended they were.

It wasn't much, but I ended up with this: "Except for one year out of state, Mick, 43, has lived his entire life in Jewett City. He is a living testament to all things familiar in the borough—he was a firefighter for the A. A. Young Jr. Hose and Ladder Co. for 20 years along with his time at the hardware store. On this Monday evening, Mick walked to the Jewett City Pizza Palace to get dinner. He lives on East Main Street and now works at Wal-Mart in Lisbon. His mother lives in Jewett City. So does three of his five sisters and two of his three brothers. 'It's home,' he said. 'It has been forever. And everybody knows everybody.'"

That was the version of the story that appeared on the Facebook page. Short and sweet. But the next twenty-four hours brought a whole lot more sweet. Readers poured in warm, loving responses to the life of Mick Gardner and what he meant to them. It was one of my favorite moments of all the stories. The next day I followed up with the following post that described their reactions; it was the only time during the project that I broke from the script like that:

"I had the privilege of interviewing Mick Gardner yesterday as he walked by my home; he was the 19th profile out of a goal of 120 profiles of people who live, work or visit the borough. Like I sometimes do with this project, I asked what made him unique. He shrugged his shoulders and said, 'I'm an ordinary, everyday person. Nobody special.' Within hours, the story reached more than 3,500 people and many posted comments that contradicted his self-image, celebrating how 'awesome' he is. It was inspiring, demonstrating once again that even so called ordinary people here are actually extraordinary to the ones who know them. Keep it up Jewett City (and beyond)!"

That reach was a relatively high number considering the target, hyperlocal audience. I know Mick's story wasn't dramatic. I'm not so sure any of the profiles I wrote were particularly Hollywood material. Still, I found each story interesting. Philippians 2:4 (NLT) puts it this way: "Don't look out only for your own interests, but take an interest in others too."

Here are a few of the readers' responses:
Small town celebrity
Mick is very polite and kind to everyone he meets. :)
So true he's always been a nice guy even in his youth
Who said you wasn't a star
One of ah kind
Awwww Mick!
That's cool Mickey you deserved to be honored
He is my friend til the end!
I see you walking everyday. Hometown Pride!
Mick is one of those rare, honest to goodness, nice guys. I've known him since he was a little kid.

And from his mother, Charlene Collins Gardner: *He is def, a icon in Jewett city!*❤

On a Saturday in March, I rushed out of the house to stop a family of three as they passed by on the sidewalk. The grandmother, fifty-five, drew a blank when I asked her what was unique about her. It's one of my favorite questions. Admittedly, it's hard to answer on the spot, especially about ourselves.

But her husband quickly filled in the silence. "She's ex-army. I like that she's skilled in weapons and guns. Compared to an 'I-broke-a-nail' girl."

Three sentences and the story moved from ordinary to fascinating just like that.

The couple, who met at a US army base in West Germany in 1979, were joined by their nine-year-old grandson. The couple was living on the edge of the borough. The husband, fifty-nine, grew up in the "ghettoes of San Francisco" with an abusive mother who shot and killed his father when he was sixteen, he said. The grandfather drove a cab in the Norwich area. He said on one occasion he gave a ride to a woman visiting the Mohegan Sun casino who was a member of the Trans-Siberian Orchestra. His next passenger was a woman he described as a heroin addict. "It's like a rolling *Jerry Springer Show*," he said. "You never know who's going to be in your cab."

The interview was again short but colorful and quotable.

Since our interview, the grandmother and I have waved to each other as I drive by in my truck. She told me once that every time she walks by my house she thinks about my invite to the small group meeting my wife and I host on Thursday nights. She never plucked up the courage to accept the invite, but I've learned there's something powerful in our simple acknowledgement of each other and the exchange of smiles and waves. The effect is a softening of the general hardness of heart that makes it a little easier to be connected to the strangers in our lives.

Anne Kudelchuk, owner of Altone's Restaurant on Main Street, attracted the biggest response of any story I wrote, garnering 235 shares. She is known for her generosity, and this quality shined through in the interview. At the time, she was set to serve Thanksgiving dinner to three hundred needy people. I interviewed her years ago for stories at the *Bulletin*, but for this moment I happened to come across her on the sidewalk because a group of people from our church were going door-to-door to deliver free pumpkin pies in several neighborhoods across the borough. She was visiting a friend.

Anne shared that week's preparation details. "No one is a bum," she said, noting she hates that term. "I try to stress we are all brothers and sisters." Anne, who has battled breast cancer, loves to give. She has hosted nearly three hundred benefit dinners. That afternoon, she delivered a bag of healthy cat food to an elderly friend whose cat was sick. Afterward, Anne planned to prepare dinner for Anne's husband and a friend she met in New York, where Anne grew up in the restaurant business in the Bronx. Anne, who was born in Italy, was the first Italian her friend ever met. Anne said her friend, who was born in Jamaica, was not only the first Jamaican she ever met, but also the first black person.

Anne is known locally for the benefit dinners. But catching her in the simple, ordinary act of kindness with the delivery of healthy cat food to a friend also touched the hearts of this project's readers, whose reactions showed what still matters to a community:

Angie I remember when I helped you take care of your mom you were so loving and you keep on giving your great

Thank you for your kindness

Anne and my aunt met at chemo and began a relationship of sharing their days and experiences. My aunt recently passed and Anne sent two trays of food to the family. She has a heart of gold.

Thank you for the benefit for my daughter Maddy we greatly appreciate the generosity and kindness

The world needs more Annies!!

I worked in valet at Mohegan sun for 11 yrs. she always came into valet, she is a very fun spirited lady always joking with the guys. Very generous!

It takes a humbled soul to serve others in need. May God bless you for all that you do.

You are one in a million... A diamond in the rough! Thank you for all you do in the community!

Annie put on a benefit 15 years ago for my daughter who was born 16 weeks premature. She has a heart bigger than this entire planet!

I met Annie at the cancer center! Her spirits were way high, she made my wife feel so good during their sessions. Wonderful woman! God bless. You look great Annie

I met Annie at my first chemotherapy treatment for lung cancer she was a breath of fresh air we clicked right away she was getting treatment as well but bringing in food for the other patients and workers at the cancer center what an earth angel she is!!!! God bless and your family Annie

I loved the reaction to another story I wrote.

Six days a week, Jeff Vowels would rush home on his break from his job at Norwich Lumber in Lisbon to spend time with his fiancé and their four-year-old son. On the day of this spontaneous interview, once again Jeff stood with Jill Nazarian as they welcomed Odin off the bus outside of their apartment at Mathewson Street. Odin, who has autism, was returning from a summer enrichment program in town. Jeff and Jill, both thirty-five, wore necklaces featuring a puzzle piece, a symbol used to raise awareness and support of autism.

"He's got an amazing personality," said Jill, who was working as a receptionist at The Spa at Norwich Inn in Norwich. But his struggles to communicate verbally would sometimes bring her to tears. Jeff said Odin doesn't struggle with most issues, such as loud noises, that are indicators of a child with autism. "What keeps him on the spectrum is he doesn't talk," he said. Jill said Odin has excellent problem-solving skills. He often showed his mother affection by kissing her on the cheek. "He's a big hugger," Jeff added. And Odin was learning to say, "I love you," for example. He would say it in syllables that his parents recognized. "It doesn't sound like, 'I love you,' but it kind of does," Jeff said. "You can see he wants it so bad," he said of Odin's desire to talk.

Jeff, meanwhile, had been in tears recently because his mother, Julie Vowels, was rushed to the hospital, and he thought she was about to die. She had been suffering bone and breast cancer. It turned out, though, that she had suffered salmonella poisoning. At the time, she was recovering in a convalescent home in Manchester. Jeff and Jill have known each other since they were twelve, attending Griswold schools together. The first time they dated it didn't work out. But they told me they had been together for about seven years. Jill said Jeff has a sharp memory. He recalled their first meeting.

"Hey, new girl," he said to her at school, and then asked her for fifty cents for lunch.

The idea of these two parents working so patiently to teach their autistic son to say "I love you" would of course never make headlines. It's too everyday. But in a harsh world, the story highlighted a sweetness and tenderness that serve as the magnet that makes our hearts stick close to a community.

Readers' responses:

With these two loving parents I'm sure Odin (sweet little boy) will continue to do well. Prayers going out for your Mom, many of us remember Julie & Greg from many years ago the 70's were a great time to grow up in JC.

Great story beautiful family. I have a daughter with autism and things will get better

This is a family I want to be friends with!

Awww hey u guys! Odin is adorable & I will be praying for a breakthrough in his development & in ur life don't need luck when u got God on ur side. Xo

This family is so amazing and loving! They are really great people who take autism head-on and in spite of it are raising a wonderful, smart little boy.

Great Story, i also have a Austic Granddaughter, You are loving and caring Parents. Prayers.

That is the most loving and touching story I've heard in a very long time and all so true. What a beautiful family and love u all!

I too have a little 5 year old guy who is nonverbal autistic. Be strong, be well and know that there are people who understand. God speed to you beating that nasty little disease of cancer.

Months later I messaged Jillian through Facebook to check on Odin's progress. She replied: *I'm so glad you asked. YES Odin can say I LOVE YOU MOMMY! And daddy also. Along with a ton more words! His progression has been amazing since we did the story, it was one of those things that could have gone either way, he could have never been able to say those words, but with hard work from everyone he works with it is able to happen. It's slow progress but it's progress and the most credit for all he accomplishes I say goes to him, he's so determined and amazes me every day!*

After lunch with the photographer one day at Dean's Corner Diner, I slid over to Mike Minarsky's table, where he had just ordered his food. When I asked if I could interview him, he answered, "Who me? Really?"

Mike told me his next stop that day was to visit Eastern Connecticut Hematology & Oncology Associates in Norwich. He was planning to give a television for the waiting room that would scroll news and advertising from Wolverine Radio, which Mike owns and operates here in the borough.

"More importantly, it will share positive words to encourage people with cancer," he said, wiping away tears.

The tears took me by surprise. But they also endeared me to this man who was willing to be vulnerable in such a public setting.

Whether it's the cancer patients at the Norwich office or the residents of Jewett City, Mike said his passion is people. "And making a difference," he said.

And it's the borough's people he has the greatest fondness for. His connection to Jewett City began when he was just months old and his parents lived for six months on Ashland Street, the same duplex he returned to just a year ago.

Mike could name the diner's previous owners dating back to when he was a boy. "I used to come here and get slush puppies," he said. After his family spent a couple of years away in New York, they returned in time for Mike to enroll in kindergarten at a former school at the church across from my house.

Mike, a 1984 Griswold High School graduate, worked at Skate-Inn in Plainfield as a teenager. His duties included playing the music, which gave his first taste of what he imagined it would be like if he landed a career in radio. His initial radio stint was at WINY in Putnam. "I was pushing buttons for two years," he said. "I never even cracked the mike." He worked at the station off-and-on for five years, but then took a job with RadioShack for thirteen years. After that, he worked for Verizon Wireless for twelve years. He lived in Meriden for seven years while working at a Verizon store near there. He and his wife, Liana, moved to a home they still own on Hill Street six years prior to the time of our talk when Mike took an opportunity to manage a new store in Waterford.

"I never wanted to leave, and I couldn't wait to get back," Mike said. "For five of those years I was trying to get back to Jewett City. I'm one of those guys who doesn't like change. I like it here. I have friends. I have business interests here now. I always called it my little Mayberry, like Andy Griffith.

"I found out these last couple of years doing this," he said, pointing across the street to the radio station, "it's not Mayberry anymore. But I still like it. It's different, but good."

Despite the benefits and insurance, Mike grew unsatisfied with his Verizon job. "I just couldn't do it anymore," he said. He left without a secure job in place. But he doesn't regret his decision.

"Walking out of Verizon and knowing I'll be alive," he said of that moment of personal victory and not fearing the future. "I am happier and more fulfilled now than I've ever been in my life."

Wolverine Radio launched two years prior to our interview as Mike contemplated the lack of hometown news. He said the television networks ignore the town unless there is an unusual human interest story or a major crime. "But there are things that happen on a daily basis that are important to a lot of people," he said.

Mike's local connections and goodwill toward the borough resulted in one particular moment he was proud of. When a house fire behind the radio station left a family homeless, Mike called Bert Surrell, owner of Surrell's Pizza & Pub on Slater Avenue, who then donated pizzas to the family for a meal. Mike then called AmericInn, a hotel on Route 138, who then provided shelter for the family.

"To me, I'm insignificant to the whole process," he said. "A piece of it, but that's it."

Mike has three children and two stepchildren—Chelsea,

twenty-five, Nicholas, nineteen, Rhiana, nine, Lakota, twenty-four, and Dane, sixteen.

Mike described himself as a mush. When he tells his youngest child she is the love of his life, he cries. And that summer when Matt MacMurray shared the news that he wanted to marry Mike's daughter, Chelsea, the tears flowed again. "He hugged me and said, 'I knew you were a cryer.'"

Certainly, Mike is not insignificant in the process or community-building, but rather an extraordinary link among neighbors in his own way.

Readers' responses:

You have heart and generosity for days. I cannot think of anyone more worthy of such a lovely tribute. It is an honor to have a friend like you!

I don't know you personally but I listen to you and read all your Facebook posts. Every town needs a guy like you. Thanks for being there for us.

I've been here all my life, I totally get what u mean, Mike!!

Speaking of neighbors, I, along with several others in town, have long been more than curious about a man whose garage is a virtual train museum. He lives just two houses up from me. I found his story to be extraordinary and one of the most interesting profiles of the entire series.

Bob Heyworth spent the first twenty-five years of his life in Canada believing his father had died in battle in World War II.

"Then one day he tapped me on the shoulder and said, 'I am your father,'" Bob, seventy-two, recalled.

Turned out his parents had a bitter divorce, and his mom's side of the family lied and told him the war story. In actuality, his father had served as a camp guard for German prisoners of war in Canada. When Bob would hang out at his friend's house across the street, the man who was also there spending time with the parents was Bob's father, watching him grow up. He remembered the look he saw on that man's face from time to time. "It was like he wanted to sneeze, laugh, or cry. But he just wanted to say, 'You are my son.'"

The two quickly developed a close relationship. His father's and uncles' experience working in railroads cemented a love for all things train-related. The seed for that passion was planted when Bob was five and living in Vanderhoof, British Columbia, which he said had a population of about four hundred people and didn't get electricity until he was seven. Twice a week, Bob would help unload the cargo trains for his grandfather's lumberyard. His grandfather on his mother's side had struck it rich panning for gold in 1900. Bob's father also use to fish and pan for gold in the Skeena River. "He hit (gold) a couple of times," Bob said.

In 1983, Bob collected his first train lantern. Now his garage at his home on Faust Street has been converted to an immaculately organized display of train memorabilia and artifacts, featuring a fully operational 1946 Fairmont rail inspector car and a model freight car that doubles as a liquor cabinet that he built himself.

"This is my little kingdom," he said. "I'm the last of my family to have some kind of railroad adventure."

Bob and his wife, Lucy, had been married forty-eight years at the time, with "no station stops in between." As a Canadian, Bob joined the US Navy during the Cuban-Missile Crisis and became a dental technician for twenty years. That training led to a career that spanned nearly fifty-four years. Retired, he was still working part time for Aspen Dental in Waterford. A job at the University of Connecticut dental school originally drew Bob and Lucy from California to Enfield, CT, before they moved to Jewett City in 2002.

Bob is licensed to operate the inspector car through the North American Railcar Operators Association. He and his father used to ride together along rail lines in New Hampshire. Bob eventually also logged eight thousand miles on one caboose and his wife logged four thousand on another.

Bob and Lucy's son died just four hours after he was born at the Naval Submarine Base in Groton. Bob said he has no doubt he will see him one day soon in heaven. He believes Jesus is the answer to any problem in life.

"God is good," said Bob, who survived colon cancer. "We all have a mission to complete."

In short, his ordinary garage, once opened, reveals an extraordinary history.

Readers' responses:

I always wondered about that house and all the train stuff. My son loved trains when he was very small and trains always make me think of him. Great story!!

Several people in this project were those in the military. Our men and women in uniform are local heroes. I met the following soldier at Subway restaurant on North Main Street after finishing my own meal. In this case, I began by focusing on Baine Sevigney, but soon realized it was his uncle's perspective that was vital to the story. The uncle paced by our table as Baine and I talked, occasionally filling in sentences for the soft-spoken soldier dressed in uniform. The uncle was full of emotion.

At his lowest point during boot camp in the US Marines, Baine was about to be demoted to another platoon, a two-week setback. So his drill instructor called Baine's uncle for motivation and put the two of them on the phone together.

"No matter what happens in life—no matter what—I love you," Tony Nigro, forty-five, of Voluntown told Baine. "But don't let those words be an excuse for you to drop out."

"Are you crying, Dad?" Natalie asked Tony as he recalled the story about Baine.

Tony, his wife, Diana, Natalie, and Baine's mom, Recina, flew down to see Baine when he graduated that February from basic training from Parris Island in South Carolina. The graduation followed the Crucible, a fifty-four-hour grueling training exercise that culminates thirteen weeks of camp. At the end, the drill instructor who had been so hard on them all put the Eagle, Globe, and Anchor, the US Marines official emblem and insignia, into the hands of each individual, an act that elicited tears from many of the recipients and onlookers.

"I was just crying," said Tony, a bricklayer. "It was unbelievable. The singing. The cadence. I can't do it justice."

Baine, twenty-four, graduated from training as a motor transportation mechanic from Camp Johnson in North Carolina the day before our spontaneous interview. Tony drove down for the special occasion and on the way home was so excited catching up with Baine that he was pulled over for speeding because he had gotten distracted.

Tony was the one to encourage Baine to join the Marines. Tony said he regretted not joining the Marines himself when he had the chance. "He's outdone me in everything with that one move," he said of Baine. Tony said he also wished he had done more as a father figure for Baine years ago, but Tony was in his twenties and didn't know how to follow through in his relationship with Baine at the time. Baine didn't know his father.

"I love him like he's my own son," Tony said. "I'd die for that kid."

Baine, a 2014 Griswold High School graduate, returned at 1:30 a.m. that day. He went to Providence, RI, to check in with his lead chain of command. Tony drove him, and Natalie joined them for the ride. Back in the reserves, Baine said it was strange to adjust to civilian life. "It's hard to talk to people," he said. But Tony sees a dramatic change in Baine for the good, starting with Baine's newfound sense of respect for himself and others as shown in simple gestures such as his politeness. He was living in Voluntown with Tony and his family at the time and said he would return to his job working in the parts department for General Dynamics in Pawcatuck.

As grueling of an experience as it was, Baine said he had no regrets about his decision to join the Marines.

"If I had to do it all over again I would," he said.

I discovered Baine's story, and the special bond he had with his uncle, after an ordinary outing to a Subway restaurant.

Readers' responses:

CONGRATULATIONS MARINE!!

Congrats,welcome home, and thank you for your service!

Congratulations Marine. Hoo rah

Semper Fi…

Leilani Rosero shared One Square Mile's photo. My baby brother is not a baby anymore :(I am so proud of him more than he will ever know! I was worried for awhile about where in life he would go and I'm so glad that Uncle Tony's (Anthony Nigro) drilling over and over and over again about joining the military worked!!!! It was a huge topic at every single holiday lol!!! And you were missed for all the holidays you were gone! The family gatherings sure weren't the same!!! I love you and miss you Baine Sevigney!!!!!!!! P.S. Even though your taller than me now and are no longer a little boy but a amazing man your still always gonna be my little brother :) I love you ❤❤❤❤

When our eyes are open, the school janitor can be a local celebrity.

Gary Frink, sixty-eight, who I interrupted on his riding mower, told me he used to enjoy sitting outside his home on Hawkins Street with his son, Steven, to watch the birds visit the feeders. Gary's street intersects mine, and I can see his house from my study window.

"He liked to watch the hummingbirds," said Gary, who was wearing a Ford hat and riding a sit-down mower.

When Steven, known as "Critter," didn't show up for work as the head custodian at Griswold Public Schools right at 7:00 a.m. on July 31, 2015—the same day as Gary's wife's birthday—his aunt across the street began getting calls from worried colleagues. Gary looked outside and saw Steven's truck still parked in the driveway. His heart sank. He went upstairs to Steven's bedroom and his fear was confirmed. Steven had suffered several health complications, Gary said, but the family believed he died of sleep apnea. He was forty-five.

"She was devastated," Gary said of Linda, his wife of forty-seven years. "She's still devastated." The loss of a child has its own particular pain, Gary said. "You always think it's going to be you first," he said.

Steven received his endearing nickname as a child from one of his friends in the neighborhood.

Gary and Linda have lived in their home for forty years. He called it the "Queen's Corner." The couple was content to stay home; he couldn't remember ever going on a vacation. "Any partying happens here," he said. The home belonged to Linda's grandfather. Linda grew up in a home across the street that was then owned by her sister. Gary also grew up in town.

He fondly recalled his thirty-one years working first as a maintenance worker at the former Norwich State Hospital, and eventually as a construction coordinator supervising thirty people at Connecticut Valley Hospital in Middletown. He took the golden handshake and retired at age fifty-five. Gary was also a member of the A. A. Young Jr. Hose & Ladder Co., the fire department across the street from his home, and retired as fire chief after thirty years of service.

Mark "Doc" Frizzell, who had recently retired as principal of Griswold High School, gave a copy of the 2016 yearbook to Gary. Inside is a tribute page to Critter, described as a man with a heart of gold.

"I never heard a bad word about him," Gary said.

One of my first jobs was as a custodial assistant for Griswold Public Schools. Critter was a supervisor. I remember him well.

Readers' responses:

Erin Patricia: Wonderful article. Critter is so very missed! Love to you all.

Erin is the principal of Griswold High School.

At the time of our street interview, Mike Verville said he biked ten miles a day in an effort to lose weight and get in shape. Most of the biking was done in one of his two recumbent trikes, or bicycles that offer laid-back riding positions.

"It's very comfortable," Mike, sixty-six, told me on his way back to his home on Ashland Street. He and his wife, Joy, had lived there since 1978. They moved here because Joy's mother was living in town.

Mike said he was in the best shape of his life as a football player at Norwich Free Academy, where he graduated in 1968. He had a hip replacement about ten years ago and stents inserted into his heart. Mike retired as a pipe fitter from Electric Boat in Groton after more than thirty years in 2014.

He and Joy have four married children and four grandchildren who were living in Eastern Connecticut. The couple first met on a blind date. "She understands me pretty good," he said.

Joy retired as a teacher's aide in Griswold due to a bad back. He said the couple has two dogs—a St. Bernard named Bo and a Newfoundland and Pyrenees mix named Aggie, after a character on the former television show *Mash*.

Mike believed the country was better at that time than it was just a few years ago, but he was concerned about the fear he said was being promoted among the political right. Looking back, I'm surprised politics didn't come up more often in conversations. Mike was reading a book about ancient Rome.

Mike was a difficult interview because it was hard to get him to talk. And believe me, I tried, with my friend and colleague, Greg, patiently waiting nearby to take the photo and my truck pulled over on the side of the road.

But here's the response, from his son:

Austin Verville: Rereading this now that I have time. All jokes aside if you ever wanted to know my Dad this is about what you could expect. Simple statements quiet responses to questions that would get more boisterous comments from others and a reference to what's important to him. Family, Ma, his dog buddies, a nice quiet ride, a good book, and a peaceful life. Exceptional people live extraordinary lives that others see as simple and normal. That's my dad love ya Pop!

Austin put it well.

There is a certain extraordinary power to a quiet, peaceable life.

Putting these stories together made me see that even people who feel they are not special need to be shown they are special to someone. Take time to hear their stories. Celebrate local heroes. Understand that common battles, if handled with grace, such as teaching an autistic child to say "I love you," resonates far beyond the family itself. And extravagant generosity always brings people closer together. Just ask Anne at Altone's.

Action Steps and Reflection:

1. Each morning, Chris Ulmer, a special education teacher in Jacksonville, Florida, spends time with his students just praising and encouraging each individual. A video that went viral shows him telling students, "You are very funny. You are very smart. You are awesome." In light of these stories of so-called ordinary people, how can you and your community pour praise on fellow neighbors, surrounding, so to speak, certain individuals with encouragement? What would it look like if communities took the time to build up the life of one person each week? First Thessalonians 5:11 (NLT) says, "So encourage each other and build each other up, just as you are already doing."

Mick Gardner

Anne Kudelchuk

Jeff Vowels and Jill Nazarian with their son, Odin

Mike Minarsky

Bob Heyworth (photo by Greg Hartzell)

Baine Sevigney, center, with his uncle, Tony Nigro, and Tony's daughter, Natalie

Gary Frink

Mike Verville (photo by Greg Hartzell)

THE WORLD SHARED IN THE POWER OF A TESTIMONY

Lesson #3: Your Community
Needs to Hear Your Story

"She used to be ashamed of her story, now she's excited to tell them about God's mercy, favor and glory." My friend posted this quote by "womenbychoice," and it's perfect for this part of my story. Christian singer TobyMac put it this way: "Your story could be the key to unlock someone else's prison. Don't be afraid to share it."

In the one square mile of your world there are no doubt stories of redemption—stories of how people overcame challenges, survived health scares, and bounced back from tragedies. In this project—and throughout my life—I have discovered testimonies of how someone encountered God's supernatural love.

They demonstrate the hope of victory in the midst of defeat.

In one example, a man who had been addicted to drugs and had prepared himself to die was rescued by an intervention that can only be described as miraculous. In a town where drugs threaten to poison the soul of the community, this story bears particular relevance and can speak to people in a more powerful way than statistics.

These stories are often untapped resources in our communities, particularly in places where the messages are so negative—you're broken, you're poor, you're defeated. The church I serve in Norwich grew tired of seeing "condemned" signs on the front doors of foreclosed homes in our neighborhood. There's been so many over the years it's as if some people believed they too were condemned, carrying a sign on the door of their hearts that shut them out of their hopes and dreams.

But that's not what we believe. We believe we are blessed. And that's the message we flooded the area with through lawn signs that read: "Blessed: Not Condemned." We borrowed from John 3:18 that says, "Whoever believes in Him is not condemned."

There is an inherent power in story—a power in hearing someone else be vulnerable. It helps me, in turn, be vulnerable, be honest about my mistakes, my failures, my weaknesses. In this process there lies a strength that tears down walls.

John Clemens, who I wrote a profile on, later joined me on a November evening at my parents-in-law's home for our cell group. I drove by in my truck and saw him standing outside his home around the corner from my own. I rolled down the window and shouted, "When are you going to take me up on my invite?" I had asked him a few times if he wanted to join me for the meetings, and although he said he would like to one day, he hadn't been able to make it so far. So he surprised me when he immediately answered, "How about tonight?"

That night Owen Upton-Pepin, who was living in the borough with his wife, Danielle, shared how he was neglected by his alcoholic father as a boy in England, where he was born. His father called his sister, Priscilla Pepin, who lives here in town, and asked her if she would care for Owen and his sister, Jennifer, if anything should ever happen to him. One week later, Owen and Jennifer discovered him dead on their couch. Owen acted out often as a child, struggled greatly in school, and wasn't given much chance for success. But he defied the odds and, among other things, ministers as a musician at our church, a turnaround he attributed entirely to the grace of God.

Five others shared their own stories of how the love of Jesus Christ transformed their lives. As we walked home, John paused before crossing the street to say he may not share our faith, but he thoroughly enjoyed hearing the testimonies. He said he had been inspired and moved by what they had to share and had not experienced anything like that ever before.

I already knew Owen's story. But there were other stories

of redemption I uncovered in my one square mile, mostly from strangers, but also from people I had come to know.

On an unusually warm day in December, I had the privilege to interview Sorel Sylvain. It had been a while since Sorel exercised by kicking a soccer ball along the streets of Jewett City, but the sixty-one-year-old Haitian native had a lot on his mind and knew he needed to get out and pray while he ran that afternoon.

Before I ever knew him, I saw him kicking a soccer ball on his run through the borough years ago. We ended up becoming close friends and then missionary companions on that 2010 trip to Haiti following what is the worst natural disaster in modern history. Before we even set foot in Haiti, we were warned of the growing dangers. People were increasingly desperate in a nation that was already the poorest in the Western Hemisphere. Riots broke out at food distribution sites. Violence grew in the makeshift camps. Police shot looters. Disease loomed. We braced for the worse. But we were surprised by hope on that trip.

Right from the first prayer meeting at the First Haitian Baptist Church of Norwich prior to our departure, Sorel reminded us we were on a mission and no mission is easy. He was right. Our only route into Port-au-Prince was via a flight that took us from JFK International Airport in New York to Fort Lauderdale in Miami to Santo Domingo, Dominican Republic. We then traveled eight hours in a car crammed with eleven pieces of luggage and ten carry-ons out of the city and through sleepy farming towns until we reached the border of Haiti. The entire journey lasted nearly thirty hours. At the border, we got out of the car while Estime, the pastor of the church, and Cynthia, one of the members, got our passports approved. Pascal Devaux, the Norwich mailman who befriended the Haitian church and joined us on the trip, recalled how a friend from his seminary days was killed on a mission trip to Burundi. Sorel answered in solemn agreement: "This is not a game. This is serious."

He first told me his testimony on the van ride to JFK International Airport in New York, startling me as halfway through his story he began to loudly praise God for all He had done in his life. Ever since, I've thought of him often and the fact that a man who God changed in such an incredible way passes by my home nearly every day as a living example of God's redemptive power. So I was more prepared than for other interviews to talk to Sorel for a story, though the interview itself was spontaneous. I caught him in a particularly painful moment of his life, as he shared the following story.

As an elder at his church, Sorel said—with tears that day outside my front door—he sometimes needs to confront a brother or sister in Christ with correction that not everyone wants to hear. Sometimes "everyone is scared to talk. They think, 'If I talk everyone is going to get mad.' But who cares if it is the truth?" And, he added, if it is said in love.

Sorel arrived in the United States in 1982 as a stowaway leaving behind harsh times at Ile La Vache, an island of Haiti. He was first detained in Miami and then sent to Puerto Rico with others in similar status for a year. Limbo and family separation created an atmosphere of desperation. Some committed suicide. Sorel was eventually permitted entry to Brooklyn, New York, to be with a relative. But his life spun out of control as he abused drugs and stole to feed his addiction.

In 1990, after one particular binge, he made his way back to the basement of an abandoned home he was living in just so he could die. He was there five days without eating, but he heard a voice in the haze of his mind that said, "This Sunday they will come for you." He attributes that voice to the Holy Spirit. That Sunday a woman was sleeping when she heard a whisper: "Get up right now. I have somebody you are going to save." She said she was prompted by God to go and seek someone who needed to be rescued. She drove to where she felt God had directed her, called out into the home in an area she had never visited, and was amazed when she heard Sorel's voice in response. She left and returned with two men from her church who cleaned him up and took him to a service where he said he committed his life to following Jesus.

Sorel, who was living just outside the borough on Monroe Street, remembered that in those early days he would walk in the "power of God" and share his testimony often on the streets. But lately his heart had been heavy, and he had started to "lose power." The run refreshed him. He had preached the night before, referring to Jeremiah 17:7–8 (NLT):

But blessed are those who trust in the Lord and have made the Lord their hope and confidence.

They are like trees planted along a riverbank, with roots that reach deep into the water.

Such trees are not bothered by the heat or worried by long months of drought.

Their leaves stay green, and they never stop producing fruit.

The Bible is the most read book in history. Here's another example of its practical popularity as the scriptures were alive in Sorel, bringing clarity into the midst of the hazy thoughts of his natural mind. And to my own mind, I will now add. Sorel didn't realize how much he encouraged me with his honesty as we talked on the sidewalk.

Readers' responses:

Mike Minarsky (he is also profiled in this book): *I saw him kicking the ball today down the sidewalk*

Great story. Thanks!

May God continue to bless him! What a powerful story thank you!

When I went back to get Sorel's permission to use his name in the book, I sat down with him and his wife in his new apartment just two streets away from me and across the basketball court and Little League complex. I asked him to elaborate on the original street interview.

"I would start by telling (people) how I had been in a mess," he said. "When I tell them I've been there, I know what I'm talking about."

His time in Brooklyn featured about five years of sleeping on the streets, breaking into cars to steal change, and selling and using crack cocaine. On one occasion, he used the drugs he was supposed to sell. He had to reckon with the dealer, who showed up at his apartment. Sorel was $100 short. "Today is going to be your last day," the dealer told Sorel. "Open your mouth." The man put the pistol in Sorel's mouth and pulled the trigger. Nothing happened. Twice more the man pulled the trigger. Still nothing happened, and Sorel escaped out the back door.

That was 1990. "It's for a reason," Sorel said. In 1996, his car burglaries and other crimes caught up with him, and he was ordered to appear in court. But the judge dismissed the charges. "You have a light in your eyes," the judge told Sorel. "The Lord saved me," he responded. "Yes, I see it in you," the judge answered. The sealed charges meant Sorel avoided deportation.

Once again, the re-telling of his testimony brought Sorel to tears, and he had to compose himself before he continued.

Another time, Sorel was eating dinner when he said he was filled with the Holy Spirit and began to cry. He felt God told him to use his and his wife's savings to build a church in Ile La Vache. But that's where his family lived; her family lived in Port-au-Prince. He was concerned his wife would think he was being unfair. So he prayed: "Would you please tell my wife what you told me." That night, she awoke from a restless sleep and turned to Sorel, who was already awake, to tell him God spoke to her and said to use their savings however Sorel deemed necessary.

On a subsequent visit, Sorel was preaching the gospel in the streets when two women who were known for disrupting other preachers through witchcraft began to harass him. He stopped preaching, turned to the women, and then commanded them in the name of Jesus to get down on the ground. They did and couldn't move. Eventually, they got up and made decisions to be followers of

Jesus. That day, fifteen people all together made the same decisions. Now about seventy-five people attend the church and about 150 students attend the adjoining school.

"When God cleans you he cleans you," Sorel said. "The purpose of God for me is to preach the word and tell people about Him."

That's a vital story for a community to hear.

I was on the lookout for the second-to-last story of this project while on a drive with Luisa. On her breaks, we usually head to a Dunkin' Donuts on Route 138 just outside of the borough but still in town. Then we drive the backroads to take in the beautiful farm scenery, including plowed fields, rows of corn stalks, and streams. On the way for our coffee, I spotted Jerry White's unmistakable red chimney van. I've known Jerry for years as a fellow member of our church. I even wrote about him once for the *Bulletin*. I had hoped to come across him without actually scheduling an interview. So after I dropped Luisa off at work, I headed back to where I had first spotted him. Fortunately, he was still there. This is what I wrote:

As far as Jerry White is concerned, each chimney job he does here in the borough and elsewhere in the region is much more than mundane work for his business—it's a living testimony to the power and love of God.

On August 11, 1994, Jerry fell twenty-three feet from a ladder on a job in Norwich and landed on his left side on an outdoor cement floor. His injuries partly included a collapsed lung, head trauma, and broken ribs. "Doctors told my family I wasn't going to live, and if I did live I'd be brain damaged," he said. Jerry was in a coma for nine days and spent eighteen days in the critical care unit at Backus Hospital in Norwich. But God did a miracle, he said.

"My church was praying around the clock for two months and God listened and moved," he said, breaking from a job cleaning an oil flue at a home on Taylor Hill Road with his son, the oldest of four children.

Jerry lives on Pleasant View Street with Laurel, his wife of forty-four years. They had five grandchildren, five step-grandchildren, and another grandchild on the way at the time of our interview.

Jerry, sixty-four, is the owner of Chimney Care Professionals. He has been cleaning chimneys for more than thirty-eight years, starting when he needed a part-time job while living in New Hampshire. He moved with his family to Jewett City in 1989. As a nondenominational minister, Jerry said he believed God wanted him to relocate in order to help a local church. Jerry also took a third-shift job for more than nineteen years as a mental health worker for the state hospital.

Jerry resumed his chimney work, even getting back on ladders, less than two months after he was discharged from the critical care unit. The only lingering problem he has from that fall is he can't fully straighten his left elbow, but nothing that hinders his work, Jerry said.

Jerry said he has seen Jesus work in him all his life, but he learned three things about God in particular during the three months after his accident: "How good He is, how faithful He is—He keeps his promises—and how He loves me personally."

For those reasons, Jerry said he can actually thank God for his fall. He referred to Romans 8:28 (NLT), which says, "And we know that God causes everything to work together for the good of those who love God and are called according to his purpose for them."

Jerry attended both the morning and evening services at the church that Sunday. And as he thought about his salvation and how good God has been to him over the years, Jerry said he was moved to tears.

Readers' responses:

I first Met Jerry & Laurel White I'm thinking around 1981 or 82 were we attended Harbinger Church up on top of Dalton Mountain in NH. We became good friends and I have never met a man more committed to GOD and his Family and Friends as he is. Praise GOD for his recovery. Though we haven't seen each other in years those memories are embedded in my heart. Praise GOD my Brother. Blessings Joe

I live near Kansas City and have been reading these stories. I am originally from Norwich, Ct. I have enjoyed them. You even did one about my Aunt and Uncle. Thank you for doing this. I love the insight. He's a wonderful man who really cares for his family and our community and he does great work!!!!

In a previous chapter I referred to the wonder of discovering people who come through Jewett City who are walking miracles. Well, here's another one. I met a woman as Luisa and I drove into the parking lot near the Little League field, one of my routine stops. Patricia Flowers was so busy trying to keep up with a little girl in her care that I almost didn't stop. I'm glad I did.

Patricia and her nine-year-old client chased butterflies that evening at the Jewett City Little League complex. They then walked and ran to the adjacent Griswold Veterans Memorial Park, where they sometimes roll down the hill together.

Four times a week, Patricia would visit her client in Jewett City as part of her job of what was one year at that time with The Arc of New London County, a nonprofit organization offering advocacy, employment opportunities, life-skills training, recreation, and more to 550 people with intellectual and developmental disabilities, according to its website.

Patricia, a 1974 Norwich Free Academy graduate, said she was grateful just to be alive. She is a breast cancer survivor since first being diagnosed with the disease in 2006. Patricia was working at Foxwoods Resort Casino when someone's bracelet caught her attention and led to a conversation with the woman who was wearing it. Turns out the woman was undergoing treatment for breast cancer, and suddenly Patricia realized she needed to have a lump examined.

Her daughter, Shea, was sixteen at the time and five months pregnant. Patricia was determined to see her grandchild born. That grandchild, Jayden, was nine when Patricia and I met. The three generations were living together in Montville. Patricia attributed her healing to God.

"There's so many things that man can't do, but God can," said

Patricia, whose son, Jay, then twenty-seven, was living in New York. "When it rains, nobody can stop the rain. When the wind blows, we can't control it."

She said God used the woman with the pretty bracelet at Foxwoods to save her life. She added that the chance meeting also demonstrated the power of awareness—she suddenly became aware of a disease that she, too, needed to address.

"I like people," she said of the work she does for The Arc and in general. "I'm here for a reason. Maybe it's to help people."

Readers' responses:

God is so good keep believing

That is also my client on Saturdays. Beautiful soul that little one. I'm glad you ran into them

What a beautiful and touching story! With Christ all things are possible.

I was invited by Griswold Pride, a local nonprofit coalition that is fighting the town's heroin problem, to speak at their meeting about the One Square Mile stories. Also in attendance was the priest of St. Mary's Church, a minister of a Christian outreach in town, and a pastor of a new church that meets at the middle school. There was a banker in the meeting who I first wondered if she was interested in hearing the presentation. On that night, in an upstairs conference room in a former mill building at Griswold Veterans Memorial Park, not only did I share stories of how people such as Sorel encountered God and His love for them, but stories of people sharing their brokenness and how they have overcome obstacles. In fact, I let the stories speak for themselves, and the redemption stories were just one of several themes I presented. At the end of the presentation, I shared how we all have walls that need to come down. The banker nodded her head, referring to herself, and was the first to speak, with tears in her eyes. "I guess what I see in all this is that people need God, right?" She asked if anyone else took the time to listen to people's stories and learn about their backgrounds. It was clear to her—doing just that is vital to the overall health of a community. Life is not at all about the amount of money we have in our bank accounts—we can't take anything with us when we die—but how we love God and love our neighbors.

English Gardner, a US track star who competed in the 2016 Olympics, put it this way: "I think that's what Christianity is all about, going through the highs and lows with God and experiencing everything that He has to offer and being able to share your story because people relate to stories," she said in an interview with Emily McFarlan Miller for Religion News Service.

Sorel's turnaround from a drug addict left to die to street preacher who spreads a message of hope tells us change is possible. Jerry's climb back onto roofs after a near-fatal fall tells us not to quit. Patricia's life-saving conversation tells us to pay attention to the details. I see God's hand on their lives. Their voices, when raised, speak life into dead places.

Actions Steps and Reflection:

1. Write your testimony. Host testimony nights in homes in your designated one square mile.
2. Communities: If truancy is a problem, share the story of a student who now regularly attends school. If heroin is a problem, share the story of someone who has found help. Don't just talk about the problems, and don't just talk about solutions in generic fashion. Give people a platform to share their victory stories.

Sorel Sylvain

Jerry White

Patricia Flowers

THE WORLD FOUND IN INTERGENERATIONAL CONNECTIONS

Lesson #4: Seek Timeless Wisdom among Our Seniors

"Is not wisdom found among the aged? Does not long life bring understanding?" Job 12:12 (NIV).

The truth is long life often does bring greater understanding. In our one square miles, it's our responsibility to seek out and honor this wisdom; in turn, we all benefit.

Jeremiah 6:16 (NIV) says, "This is what the Lord says: 'Stand at the crossroads and look; ask for the ancient paths, ask where the good way is, and walk in it.'"

We as a nation undoubtedly stand at a crossroads. Instead of being so impressed with ourselves and our technological advances, we could use some old-fashioned advice, some old-fashioned direction. Or maybe it's better to say timeless advice and timeless direction. Not all change is healthy change.

How do we get it?

We ask. Ask is a small word that produces great results—if we ask the right people. In our search for wisdom, we will find it among many of our seniors who have learned life's lessons through various hardships. And as we ask we will strengthen communities through empathy with seniors. What kind of society ceases to honor our elders and leaves them in islands of loneliness?

My great-grandmother—we called her Baba—was a Russian Jew who lived to be 101. When I was a teenager and visited my grandparents in Milford, Connecticut, with my family for

Thanksgiving, there were times when just she and I would be left at the table after dinner was over. In those moments, she liked to repeat the same story of the time she first came to the United States and a principal grabbed her by the hand and gave her a personal tour of the school. "Me—a Jew," she would tell me, reaching across the table to grab both of my hands to emphasize how dramatic it was for her because such a thing was unheard of where she was from. She'd get so excited that she would speak in Russian. I learned so much about the importance of welcoming others from listening to her telling this story and many others, including the persecution her family suffered from the pogroms and of her joy of the first time she saw the Statue of Liberty on her voyage here.

In my one square mile were three gems—Norman "Mr. GHS" Gileau and his voice of wisdom; Mama Betty and her quick wit even at 102; and a World War II veteran who still cried at the thought of the horrors of war. And another couple, two more gems, reminded me about one of the most important lessons—the brevity of life.

Norman Gileau is an esteemed town elder and one of the few interviews I actually scheduled. He was eighty-six at the time of our meeting.

Norman was my former high school principal who I saw occasionally driving by my house. I never realized he was my neighbor from just two streets away. When I called him to ask if I could stop by with a photographer, he remembered me right away even though I had graduated twenty-five years ago and we had only bumped into each other a few times since then. "Cousy," he said, referring to the nickname he gave me in high school after Bob Cousy, a point guard who played for the Boston Celtics from 1950–63. He even remembered why he gave me that nickname, saying I had played a scrappy, hustle style of ball reminiscent of the late Celtic great. It didn't matter that I was actually a bench player; it still made me feel like a superstar. He had a special way of doing that.

His story drew an overwhelming response. I didn't just focus on his career—I focused on his life, and in the process uncovered a tender moment involving his wife. The interview became emotional as he fought back tears sharing this account:

Norman said he can remember in vivid detail the moment he first saw the girl who would later become his wife—the same woman he cried over that week we talked as she lay in a hospital bed, temporarily disoriented and noncommunicative from a series of what is sometimes known as ministrokes. "The first time I laid eyes on this girl she was ten and I was ten," he said from his home of forty-eight years on Russell Street that Friday. "She was this pretty little blonde girl."

Norma was visiting family across the street from his home in Danielson. Five years later, he saw Norma again while working as an usher at a theater in Danielson. Then, during his senior year at Killingly High School, she moved from New Hampshire into town. Initially, she took a romantic interest in another student, the class president. "But on graduation night we went in the same car on the way—I remember this like yesterday—to Richard's Dairy in Putnam. From that day on we became a couple," he said. They married in 1952. She had been living at Villa Maria Nursing and Rehab Community in Plainfield the last two-and-a-half months.

Norman retired after thirty-one years as principal of Griswold High School in 1989. He and his wife have seven children and eighteen grandchildren. He laughed when he tried to recall the exact number of great-grandchildren—eight, he said. "My family is the best thing that ever happened to me," he said.

In September 2013, his grandson, Trevor Marttila, died at age twenty in a motorcycle accident soon after getting engaged. Trevor, a former Marine, never stopped showing public affection for his grandfather even as an adult. "He'd give me a hug and peck on the cheek," Norman said as he welled up with tears. "He didn't care who was around or who was watching. He was going to do this. That kid was so special. You shouldn't say you have a favorite grandson, but to be honest with yourself you do. Even though I love them all."

From his study, Norman described his biggest concern these

days. "It's not about World War III or anything like that," he said. "It's about what is going to happen to all these young people who are involved in chemicals, in heroin. How are they going to achieve happiness? Nobody is immune to this," he said, acknowledging a relative has battled an addiction.

He offered a piece of advice for today's generation. "For kids to honor their parents would be one of the best things they can do," Norman said, although he said he realized many children suffer from absentee parents. "It's one of the commandments, brought down by Moses." That quote makes me immediately think of the Ten Commandments inscribed in a monument outside St. Mary Church on North Main Street.

It's worth reading several of the reactions online to get a sense of what Norman means to the community.

Readers' responses:

What a wise man!

Always loved Mr. Gileau. He used to call me "Smiley" when I was in high school. Lovely man with a lovely family. I hope his wife will be okay. Sending prayers 🙏✨🙏✨

An old friend of mine. We did little league together in 19 years i learned much. He was full of info and wisdom. A good friend. He looks great.

This man was a wonderful mentor to me as a transfer in student in the 10th grade. He always went out of his way to make me feel welcome. Great choice for your article!

Mr. GHS! Mr. Gileau, you have such a very special place in all of our hearts. Griswold is lucky to have you. Prayers for Mrs Gileau as well.

I remember him as my principal has always been a fair and kind man. The very best principals I had, and I love the love story. You don't hear of those in today's generation.

Great man. I remember him fondly. I still have a hand written note stored away that he sent congratulating me on an athletic award back in high school.

Character, kindness, and empathy Mr. Gileau has shown many generations of young people how to live in this crazy world with the integrity he exemplifies. Thank you for the stories about his wife and grandson, and prayers for the Gileau family.

I was fortunate enough to have Mr Gileau for 3 of my 4 years at GHS- his love for us was so obvious- he would stand in the hall and praise kids while changing classes, he would sing to me, he would take over the cafeteria once in awhile & make us a special lunch- I have such wonderful memories of this gifted man. Educational excellence- God bless!

Mr. G was the toughest yet most kindest man i knew. tougher than my own parents. but i know he was like that because he saw potential in me. i was a wild thing in the early 70's. he saw my talents in music and encouraged me to be a music teacher. i chose to be a firefighter. God bless you and your fam. Mr. G.

Throughout the project, I had planned to visit the town's senior center. When I finally did, Tina Falck, director of the Griswold Senior Center, pointed me right away to the center's most active member—Elizabeth Mentillo. Her personality immediately shone through as we sat together at a dining table.

Better known as Mamma Betty, Elizabeth is 102 "and three quarters," Elizabeth said at the time with a laugh. At the time of this writing, she had recently celebrated her 103rd birthday.

Elizabeth was once again at the Senior Center on Soule Street in the borough that evening. The center hosted an open house and shared its vision for a new 13,000-square-foot facility.

"I come here every day for company," she said. "I'd like to see them get a new senior center, so I'm backing them up."

Elizabeth grew up in Stamford and lived there until about eleven years ago, when her husband died and she decided to live with her daughter, Betty Knox, in Griswold. Elizabeth and her husband, William, used to own a summer cottage at Pachaug Pond. When Betty divorced she moved here to run the cottage, giving Elizabeth her permanent connection to this town.

"How can I put it?" she asked. "I came from a big city into nothing. Stamford is a bedroom to New York. It's a big change."

Elizabeth and William were married for nearly seventy years, a relationship that began with a blind date. He was a tool-and-dye maker.

"We got along well," she said. "We had our occasional fallout, but it never lasted very long. We just got up in the morning and we were friends again."

They had two children. Her son died two years ago. "I've never been able to cry," Elizabeth said of his death, momentarily filling with tears. "Don't ask me why. I'm the one who if I saw a stranger cry I'd cry with them."

Elizabeth has four grandchildren and four great-grandchildren. She said she worked since she was thirteen, spending most of her employment days as a pharmacy clerk.

Elizabeth's motivation in life is "just to see my family happy."

Soon after our interview, my grandmother, Barbara Davis, died. Grandma Davis once lived with my family for several years and was living with my wife's parents here in Jewett City at the time of her death. At the funeral service, I was pleasantly surprised to turn around in my seat and see Mama Betty, her daughter, and another regular from the senior center in attendance. Turns out they had befriended Grandma Davis when she visited the center. And now we celebrated her life together.

I had no idea, of course, that Mama Betty was a close friend of my grandmother's at the time of our interview. And that just underscores my point—we expand our world when we open our hearts and let others in.

Readers' responses:

Love Mama Betty with her beautiful smile and personality. Many blessings.

Renee Asmar: I LOVE this beautiful and inspiring Betty, and enjoyed many occasions in her presence. God's continued Blessings abundantly flow upon Betty and her gifted daughter. ❤️🤍🌷💐🎶🎵🎶🎶🎵👭👩‍👧

So proud to call her great grandma!!

One afternoon I drove by two men working under the hood of a car near my house. I circled back and immediately found a subject who was eager to tell his story. Albert Lockwood straightened up from his car and after I briefly introduced the project he launched into what was obviously an oft-told personal account of his time in World War II. He and his son-in-law, Robert Rivard, were checking the fluids in Albert's car.

"I was in World War II you know. Let me show you something," he said before going inside Robert and Patricia Rivard's home on Lenox Avenue, where he was staying. On a wall in the living room was a glass case with Albert's military photo, seven medals, and discharge papers.

In a matter of just a few minutes, he had invited me inside his son-in-law and daughter's home, where he was staying, so he could show me his medals and pull out a well-worn scrapbook. His daughter welcomed me warmly and set up a tray in front of me to place the book on as Albert and I sat side-by-side on their living room couch. And to think we were perfect strangers just moments ago.

I ended up with the following story that included pointing readers to the US Holocaust Memorial website. I was particularly glad about that.

Albert Lockwood talks fast about his World War II experiences except when he comes to one particular moment just after the war ended.

"I'm going to talk to you about the worse time," he said, slowing down and briefly clearing his throat. "They made us go through the Buchenwald death camp. I can't even talk about that. They did that to make us hate the Germans."

Albert, ninety, served as a demolition man in General Patton's Third Army in Luxembourg and fought in the Battle of the Bulge. As a combat engineer, he helped build and reconstruct bridges for infantry to pass over, and he helped build barracks for Germans

POWS. Buchenwald was one of the largest concentration camps in Germany.

Albert has lived in Maine since 1978, but was visiting family in the region indefinitely where he had longtime roots. He lived variously in Griswold and Plainfield before moving north.

"We all look up to him," said Patricia, one of eight children from his first marriage. He also has a stepson from his second marriage. He said he visits the gravesite of his second wife, Lucy, at Pachaug Cemetery every week that he is here.

Albert was born and raised in North Stonington, moved to Voluntown, and attended Griswold High School before dropping out a week before his sixteenth birthday. He had contracted mumps, and when he recovered he went to work to support his family.

He was drafted into the war and served in the US Army from March 31, 1944, to May 11, 1946. His battalion was preparing to take the fight to Japan when he got the news. "Then Truman dropped the bomb," he said. "We didn't have to go."

After the war, Albert went on to build dozens of homes in the area, buying most of his lumber from the former A. D. Tripp Lumber Co. in Jewett City.

Albert was among the local veterans, first responders, and others honored at the town's first-ever Heroes Day, held a month earlier in September at the Griswold Veterans Memorial Park.

Readers' responses:

God Bless this generation and God Bless America

His stories should be told. They're very interesting! Gotta share this

We are very thankful for his service. There aren't many World War II veterans living. My 95 yr. old uncle in Mn is another who served in 6 major battles. God Bless them & all our veterans!

God bless you sir and thank you for your services and everything you've done

Imo this is the best story in this series. God bless both of these men for their service to this country. They don't make them like that anymore.

I could've stayed for hours. Albert wanted me to. And I could've written so much more. But I tried to keep the stories short to match readers' online attention spans. Still, even the highlights of his life moved me deeply.

Nearly four months after this interview, Albert died at age ninety-one. I learned about it from his daughter's Facebook post. The obituary noted he had nine children, twenty-nine grandchildren, sixty great-grandchildren and twenty-seven great-great-grandchildren.

As a reporter, I had the privilege of interviewing a World War I veteran. He told me of the time he rescued a fellow soldier who had been entangled in barbed wire. He told me of how he suffered from a mustard gas attack. And, over the years as a local reporter, I wrote about veterans of World War II, including survivors of the attack on Pearl Harbor, Vietnam War, Iraq, and Afghanistan, all in my town or nearby. Think of all the amazing stories of heroism and courage and service that are in your neighborhoods!

You know what else a conversation with an elder will help you understand? That time is short, which is no small lesson.

On the day I interviewed Sherry Budz, it was her seventy-first birthday. A recent stroke made it difficult for her to speak, but she had no problem smiling.

"I've had a good life," she said.

She and her husband, Robert, sixty-seven, often have breakfast at Dean's Corner Diner on Main Street, where they like to sit at the outdoor table when the weather is warm enough for the benefit of their dog, Toby. That day was no different except they used a gift certificate her sister gave her that Thursday for her birthday. The same sister, Debbie Rosacker of Moosup, tied balloons to her car that morning.

Robert and Sherry had been married for forty-eight years when we spoke, first meeting through a mutual friend. Robert was originally from Hanover in Sprague and Sherry was from Fitchville in Bozrah.

"She was making more money than I was," said Robert of his

wife's job at a convalescent home and his at a dealership. "She was making eighty dollars (a week), and I was making fifty dollars."

Robert took a job as a laundry truck driver that was vacated by his father-in-law's retirement and received a pay increase to $100 a week. He ended up working in that business—it's now run by Aramark—for forty-one years. She worked at the Courtyard by Marriott in Norwich.

The couple had lived in a home on Donald Street for forty-one years. Their daughter, Penny Kelly, was living with her husband, Patrick, in Bristol and was a teacher at the Connecticut Aerospace and Engineering in Windsor.

Robert and Sherry 's granddaughter, Katie, was a nineteen-year-old sophomore at Western Connecticut State University in Danbury at the time. "She loves drama, singing, opera," Robert said.

Robert has also faced health problems, requiring a stent in his heart and then the removal of his adrenal glands. At the time, Penny was a researcher at the science department at the University of Connecticut. In her research, she discovered Robert was one of sixteen people worldwide to suffer bone growth in his adrenal glands. Had she not discovered the reason why his blood pressure wasn't responding to the heart surgery or medications, his situation could've proven to be fatal.

"You learn mortality," Robert said. "You learn anything can happen at any time. You can be the biggest person with the most money, but you can be gone real quick."

One of Robert and Sherry's biggest joys was tracking the achievements of their granddaughter. He pulled out a program he kept tucked away in his bag to show she won a recent award. She overcame autism as a child to earn a lifetime achievement award for her work in drama.

"She's been in over thirty plays," Robert said. "She wants to be on Broadway. She has a terrific singing voice. She's worked at the Warner Theatre in Torrington."

"I keep everything she does," Robert added. "I have books from all her plays."

Readers' responses:

Jillian Nazarian (also profiled for this project): *Great story, I often see you guys and your dog at Deans ! Happy birthday.*

As I passed you by in the red car, I had thought to myself "I wish I had time to stop for a bite". Cute dog! Then drove on. So it's no surprise to find you guys in the SPOTLIGHT. Good luck to you both. 🐰🐶. *HAPPY BIRTHDAY!!*

Philip Michael Flowers: Happy Birthday! I have seen you both a few times at Dean's.

As another postscript, I caught up with Robert and Sherry at Dean's Corner for their permissions. I told Robert I was going to highlight his lesson on mortality. Turns out the day before I reunited with them he had been to the funeral of a friend who died suddenly of a heart attack. Then he told me a longer story about his uncle. The uncle was a truck driver in a convoy. One day, the rest of the drivers waited for him to leave the parking lot to follow, but the truck wasn't moving. The other drivers beeped and called him on his phone but no answer. Finally, someone opened his door and he fell out dead. He had a heart attack. And here I see once again it's vital to do our best not to take life for granted. "Don't brag about tomorrow, since you don't know what the day will bring" (Proverbs 27:1 NLT).

In March 2017, I went to a second funeral in less than a month. Something happened there that I'll never forget. Before the service even started, an aunt grabbed the mike and passionately challenged the men to get on the righteous path and break the cycle of needless, early deaths. Made me think of the scripture that says we can learn more at a funeral than at a lifetime of parties and celebrations because "death is the destiny of everyone; the living should take this to heart" (Ecclesiastes 7:2 NIV). Luisa and I took a drive afterward, took time to appreciate our moments together. Life is short. Life is a journey. If there's nothing more hopeless and inevitable than death, then there's nothing more full of hope than the gospel. I shared a brief message at that funeral: Jesus conquered death. He is the righteous path to eternity the aunt was talking about.

The stories above all illustrated a simple need in our communities—the need to listen to our elders, to hear their stories, to consider the lessons they've learned. It takes time. But make time! We need to identify these local heroes, give them a platform—in our schools, our homes, our churches—to speak to a younger generation that suffers confusion and the loss of a sense of direction and to create cross-generational bonds to combat loneliness and more. Don't wait until someone dies to celebrate his or her life or glean from his or her wisdom!

Action Items and Reflection:

1. When was the last time you made time to sit and talk with a senior? What prevents many of us from taking this step? What are we missing out on by not engaging seniors this way?
2. Call your local senior center and ask if a resident would like to join you for dinner at your home or if you can stop by and listen to his or her story.
3. Call your local Veterans of Foreign War post and offer to take a veteran out to breakfast or for a coffee.

Norman Gileau (photo by Greg Hartzell)

Elizabeth "Mamma" Betty (left) and Betty Knox

Albert Lockwood (right) and Robert Rivard

Robert and Sherry Budz

THE WORLD FOUND IN THE BEAUTY OF MANY RACES

Lesson #5: Make Race Part of the Conversation

Rebeca Morales' journey to Jewett City, and what turned out to be her brief stay here, began in Ecuador, where she was born.

She felt welcomed in the borough, but not so much when she arrived to a town in Pennsylvania from Ecuador at age eight.

"The first year was horrible. You didn't understand anything, and nobody understood me. I was bullied. I lived in a community where people were really racist," she said.

Specifically, groups of students would push her to the ground and kick her. She would pretend she was sick just to avoid school.

I met Rebeca, along with her eleven-year-old son, at the playground near the Jewett City Little League Park. I remember that moment well because storm clouds were quickly gathering as I snapped their photo.

Rebeca would prove to be one of several people to bring up the topic of race without being directly asked and to eventually serve as a subject of guided conversations, or trainings, on race we held with a group of parents, educators, and community leaders in town. Their stories come later in this chapter.

That is one of the more surreal moments of this initiative. Because of the project, I found myself thrust into the midst of a national discussion on race at a time when tensions surrounding race relations were at a dangerous high. Unfortunately, 2016 became known as the year of division with news commentators dubbing our country the Divided States of America. We weren't just divided politically—Republican versus Democrat, Trump supporters versus

Trump haters, conservatives versus liberals. We were divided along racial lines. And for a country undergoing rapid change in its racial and ethnic makeup, that's no small matter. There's simply no excuse for it.

To tell you how I went from interviewing passersby outside my front door to a national Facing Race conference in Atlanta with a record crowd of more than 2,000 participants, I will begin with Kevin Skulczyck, who at the time was the town's first selectman and the Republican candidate for Connecticut state representative in the 45th district (he eventually won the seat). He was the one to recruit me to serve as chairman of a newly formed equity and social justice subcommittee in town. I had approached him in general about the One Square Mile project on a business level, but our friendship began because his daughter is friends with my two daughters. He drove them to school every day, and Taylor, his daughter, joined us on family drives and other outings.

Personal connections, by the way, really do matter in life. We need one another.

Kevin loves to use social media as a platform for his political messages. He helped launch Griswold Now!, a closed Facebook group with more than 3,500 members. And it was under his watch that Wolverine Radio launched a station on Main Street.

The subcommittee is part of Families and Community First Griswold, which is a collaborative of town, school, and community leaders funded by the William Caspar Graustein Memorial Fund in Hamden, Connecticut. While I was in the midst of writing the series, the foundation changed its mission to "achieve equity in education by working with those affected and inspiring all to end racism and poverty."

I had shared with Kevin that I believed Jewett City would soon see a vital upturn in ethnic and racial diversity and that, instead of reacting to this demographic trend, we should get out in front of it to help foster integration and unity. The stories illustrated the point and made it increasingly evident that the people of Jewett City no longer looked like they did even just a few years ago. One Square Mile, we agreed, could be used as a springboard into courageous conversations about race and poverty in town.

Kevin likes to say he talked me into it. And it's true—he was persuasive after I had initially declined the offer in light of other commitments. He began to win me over though as we drove together on November 12, 2015, to a Graustein reconvening of educators and leaders across the state who had attended an equity summit in Los Angeles. At the meeting, organizers shared written comments of participants' reactions to the summit. I took notes of the ones that stood out to me. One wrote: "When people are talking about immigration we can't segregate conversations about wages or racism. They all tie together." Another said: "Very sad how much where you are born affects your opportunities." And still another wrote about the tenor of Black Lives Matter, quoting a reverend: "The faith community kept quiet while the criminal justice system grew. We need an act of repentance." Two others underscored the point of this project and helped convince me I was on the right path: "Make sure the real stories are being told." And, we have a "need for community conversations to raise/keep alive the issue and generate strategies."

The word *repentance* especially stood out to me.

In my capacity as one of five police chaplains in Norwich, I attended a community conversation in that city called "Race, Policing, and Violence." We broke into small groups, and I joined the community engagement breakout. We talked about the lack of respect and the general breakdown of society. I said we need a whole lot more of God's love, and a man sitting next to me said, quite loudly, "You got that right." The groups reconvened, and in the recap I found myself writing the word *repentance* down in my notes. It may be considered an old-fashioned word, but I was thinking of all the pride, bitterness, and resentments we have that fuel the sin of racism and how we need to turn in the opposite direction from these destructive attitudes. Dave Holland, a friend and deacon from another church in Norwich, came over to my table to say goodbye just as I was writing that word down. It turned out we were both thinking of John the Baptist, whose singular message was to repent. That gave him goose bumps. Maybe we need a citywide day of repentance, I thought. A day of forgiveness? A day to put things right with God and one another? Seriously, though, what would happen if we stood in unity in our one square miles and said I forgive my neighbor for every offense? After a seventy-four-year-old man in Ohio was shot and killed on his walk home from an Easter lunch—a crime recorded by the killer live on Facebook—I was moved by his three children who said in a CNN interview that they completely forgave the murderer. That was more powerful than revenge.

That night at the community conversation, in the introduction, Gregory Perry, another pastor in the city, said listening was at a premium in the country. It's easy to talk with people who are friendly, he said. "The problem is we talk *at* those who aren't," he said. He was right.

For the opening ceremony at the Facing Race conference a year after the Graustein convening, and just days after the election, a woman greeted the participants by singing in rhythmic tones, "What is your dream today?" She answered in return. "Joy. Freedom." The atmosphere was spiritual, activist, partisan. And tense. It didn't take long to call out the elephant in the room. It began with Mary Hooks, campaign coordinator of Southerners on New Ground, saying it was "time to avenge the suffering of our ancestors." Rinko Sen, president of Facing Race, took if further and said postelection week was a "prefascist moment." There was obvious pain in the room, and the villain was Donald Trump. Meanwhile, a *USA Today* headline that weekend read, "Rise in racist acts follows election," and featured one such act of graffiti in a Minnesota bathroom that read #whitesonly, #gobacktoafrica.

Michelle Alexander, acclaimed author of the New Jim Crow Laws, and Alicia Garza, founder of Black Lives Matter, were among the speakers. Keynote speaker Roxanne Gay, a feminist writer, said with gleeful irreverence that she rejected the notion of anyone telling her to get behind the new president. "We need to infiltrate. Run for office. Get on the inside." She said Democrats need to run someone who will win the next election. "Even if it's the devil," she said. And the audience laughed. I was troubled, however, by the tone of it all and the strain of this particular dream that seemed to demonize others even while boasting about inclusiveness.

Jose Antonio Vargas, another featured speaker who shot to fame after coming out as an undocumented immigrant, declared: "We are in a civil war." He said white reporters he used to work with often told him we are in a postracial society because of President Barrack Obama. The audience snickered at the assessment. Jose cited stats on the white person becoming the minority. "That should be a beautiful transition," I thought. But all I sensed was defiance and hostility. Jose dared us to "Define American," which is also the name of his new media organization. At the time, Jose was planning a video series on straight white Americans, who he said don't want change and aren't ready for it. He said the audience was his family, not like when he visits Tea Party conservatives. They laughed. He asked pointed questions: Why is it that when a white person migrates, it's courageous, manifest destiny, but not for a brown person? Why is it that goods and services—iPhones for example—move more freely into the United States than people? Is that because money matters more than people? And what does American foreign policy—imperialism and colonialism—have to do with the chain of movement and restriction on immigrants of color?

The audience ate it all up. Despite my concerns, I found some of the points valid. I felt so strongly that I was in the right place at the right time, guided there to observe and to later speak about what I learned in future talks. Still, I found myself more inspired by the in-between moments of the conference, such as at breakfast when Vicki Gallon-Clark of Connecticut happened to sit next to me and began silently praying before eating. "We all have one enemy," she said after we struck up a conversation. "The devil. It's not each other... We should all understand that we are all God's children."

Vicki used her own personal experience to back up her point. She said when our hearts are transformed, we no longer look at others through our own eyes and biases. "When we look through the eyes of Jesus, it removes the bitterness and the hatred."

As a matter of fact, that echoes the eloquent declarations of Martin Luther King Jr., who was born in the city in which we had convened. "Only through an inner spiritual transformation do we gain the strength to fight vigorously the evils of the world in a humble and loving spirit," Dr. King said. For some sad reason, people conveniently forget about Dr. King's spiritual motivation in recalling his legacy. But in his sermon "Transformed Nonconformist," Dr. King said individuals need to have a "new birth" experience in Jesus by opening our hearts to God. Indeed, this is unashamedly the window through which I view the world. Dr. King's dream is unfinished. But Jesus Christ, before He breathed His last on the cross, cried out, "It is finished." He fully paid the price of our sin, and now we can know Him and forgiveness even as we forgive others. Racism is one such sin. When Jesus reached out to the woman at the well, it shocked her because she was a Samaritan and He was a Jew and both groups weren't supposed to mix. Jesus broke down the barriers of hate. He demonstrated shocking love. And when He told the disciples to go into all the world, He said to make sure they spread His message to Jerusalem where they were staying (remember some scholars say the walled area of the city was one square mile) and to Samaria, Judea, and the uttermost parts of the world. Samaria? That was revolutionary in itself. Samaritans and Jews had hundreds of years of open hatred and hostility for each other. And yet, in a true sign of racial reconciliation, it was in Samaria that many churches were planted.

On the last day of the conference, I walked to the nearby Center for Civil and Human Rights where I took in the Civil Rights Movement gallery, featuring exhibits about the Jim Crow laws, Brown vs. Board of Education, Rosa Parks, the Montgomery bus boycott, and the Woolworth's lunch counter sit-ins. Each exhibit was like a drum beat, taking me back in solemn reflection to a not-so-distant past where unspeakable horrors were committed against black Americans. So much hatred, so much evil in this world, I thought.

There was the exhibit featuring the "four little girls" who were killed in a church in Birmingham by a bomb right after the March on Washington. There was the story of the crossing of the Edmund Pettus Bridge, where six hundred participants marched only to be met with tear gas and police beatings. The march itself was organized in response to a man who was beaten, shot, and killed by police as he was trying to protect his grandfather and mother.

In his Letter from Birmingham Jail, Dr. King said he was tired of waiting for change. As I walked through the rest of the gallery, I carefully read other quotes by Dr. King that captured his prophetic voice and taps into the spirit of One Square Mile. Like this one: "Through our scientific and technological genius we've made of this world a neighborhood. And now through our moral and ethical commitment we must make of it a brotherhood. We must all learn to live together as brothers—or we will all perish together as fools," he said.

This quote in particular nearly perfectly sums up the purpose of this initiative: "People fail to get along because they fear each other; they fear each other because they don't know each other; they don't know each other because they have not communicated with each other."

Earlier in the conference, a workshop on "Achieving Racial Equity Initiative: Changing Landscape in California" had pointed out that in 2040, the majority will be people of color. The presenters went on to discuss policy and data as it related to institutional and structural racism. But the workshop noted the idea that the data and the numbers need to be related to human experiences in order to inspire real change.

Back in my hotel room, with expansive views of Atlanta, I took time to read in Acts 10:34–35 (NLT) about the apostle Peter's revelation: "I see very clearly that God shows no favoritism. In every nation he accepts those who fear him and do what is right." No partiality includes no favorites among races.

Back home, the urgent need of racial reconciliation and the sin of racism became apparent over the course of the one year it took to write the profiles.

Tucked away in one of the 120 profiles was a statement that touched on this concern and demonstrated the need to dig deeper. One Friday night, four members of the extended Patel family helped renovate a deck of a relative's home on East Main Street, two houses down from my house. One of the men moved directly to Jewett City from Gujarat, India, in 2009. He said he thinks about his native country "all the time, every day." Homesickness hits him particularly hard during prayers and just before bed. The man, who is Hindu, had other family members who were still living in India, including his parents.

He said his happiest moments are when his family in the area attend temple either in Middletown, Connecticut, or Oxford, Massachusetts. The downside of life here takes place at his job at a gas station in Jewett City.

"I see racism at the store," he said, referring to customers. "People throw money on the counter and not in my hand. Or at my face. Makes me feel bad."

Readers' responses:

Nearly all of us were new to this country originally. Hang in there and smile. The good people will smile back and treat you decently. They're the ones that are worth getting to know anyhow.

I appreciated the reader's feedback. It makes me wonder, though. What advice would we, and should we, give to someone who has experienced such blatant animosity?

The idea that someone would throw his or her money at a worker just a few streets away from my home was obviously disturbing. But this Indian family wasn't the only one to speak up about an undercurrent of racial challenges and tension.

In July, I interviewed a couple who were here on a two-week visit from San Pablo, California. The woman found out that week she was pregnant with their child. The man, twenty, had visited the area several times growing up. His grandparents were living in Voluntown and other family members were living in Jewett City and Norwich. They visited this time because they wanted to encourage his aunt, who was battling breast cancer. They were staying with her at her home in the borough.

The couple had gone to Mohegan Sun casino for the first time and were considering going to Sailfest, a summer festival in New London that attracts more than three hundred thousand people. But he preferred his typical outing when he's here. "I just like swimming and fishing," he said. "Out there (in California) there's no fresh water."

At the time, the woman, twenty-one, had just two daughters, two and one. She and her boyfriend met on a dating website. He was working with his father in construction, "mostly plumbing and digging holes."

As we stood on the sidewalk along Main Street outside Dean's Corner Diner, the man said he feels his race stands out here, drawing stares.

"I'm Pacific Islander, Native American, French and a little Asian," he said. The woman said she is Puerto Rican and Filipino.

The boyfriend shared another story about his experience at a local pool hall and bar where it became clear to them, in one way or another, that they were not welcomed. I don't know if that was the reality. But it was certainly their perception. And that matters. And it's worth talking about.

Readers' responses:

Congrats on the lil one. Prayers for his Auntie. As for stares probably just because they are new faces. Small towns a new face stands out. In Cali I would imagine there are a lot more people and anyone would stand out less. Enjoy our summer spots.

When I first asked Mike Mickens if I could interview him,

he was getting ready to leave for an errand and asked me to come back another time. When I returned on July 5, Mike, thirty-four, said as a "six-foot-two, three-hundred-pound African American," he suspected some people here are afraid of him. "They'd be surprised that I'm friendly," he said. In Brooklyn, NY, where Mike lived until he was fifteen, he fit right in, he said.

Mike quickly clarified there's a side to him that is fiercely protective when it comes to his two-year-old daughter, Anastasia. In fact, he had considered moving even "deeper into the woods" from his condominium on Brown Avenue because of drug problems he had heard about in the borough.

He had lived in Jewett City for about eight years. A neighbor drove by as he washed his cars, beeped, and waved hello.

"I can be in a neighborhood full of Spanish, or full of Asians, or full of Caucasians," he said. "No matter where I am, I adapt."

He and his wife, Izzy, had been married for fourteen years. They lived just a mile or two from each other in Brooklyn but didn't meet until later in life when they took jobs at Mohegan Sun. Mike's parents bought a house in Montville so he and his sister could move away from the dangers of city life. Mike is a 1999 Montville High School graduate. He played varsity football all four years.

Mike originally wanted to be a state trooper, but he didn't pass the test. He carried on working at Foxwoods Resort Casino and now wants to be a state corrections officer.

Anastasia is named after Izzy's grandmother. Mike later learned he had a great-great-grandmother with the same name. Mike spent about two hours cleaning "candy and sticky stuff" left behind from Anastasia in two of his cars.

"They talk about the terrible twos. But she doesn't have that," he said. "Every morning she wakes me up. And every night she gives me a kiss, a hug, and a high-five."

She waved to him from the window of their home. Izzy, meanwhile, kept urging her husband to finish up and spend time inside with the family.

I have used Mike's story about people being afraid of him just because he's a big, black man several times in discussions about race. At the end of the day, much of what gets in the way of racial reconciliation is an abiding sense of suspicion and fear of others. Open, honest dialogue helps soften perceptions and soften hearts.

Readers' responses:

He should try again for the state police. Keep trying. The state needs more nice friendly troopers.

When I met Alisha Martin and her niece, Madison, outside my home we didn't talk about race. But we have stayed in touch in person and on Facebook. It's Alisha's Facebook posts that opened my eyes to her concerns about race, particularly one on October 5, 2016, that started with an angry face emoji and "feeling pissed off" mood description. She was upset that "white kids" were calling her daughter a racial slur. "Looks like I'm going to have to find out who parents are and get in contact with them personally!"

I called her that afternoon and invited her to become part of the equity and social justice team. She readily agreed. More specifically, I asked her to participate in a training on race and poverty that was supported by a $20,000 Graustein grant. Initially, as chairman of the social justice subcommittee, I was asked to advise the collaborative in the selection of pre-approved national consultants provided by the foundation. But another one of the parents of my daughters' friends proved to be a vital connection. That mother, Terrlyn Curry Avery, and I were already acquainted when we bumped into each other at a vigil held for the fallen Dallas police officers outside of City Hall in neighboring Norwich. That evening on July 12 I had the privilege to serve as one of five chaplains for the Norwich Police Department. Terrlyn, a licensed psychologist, handed me a business card that advertised her expertise in providing training on race relations. She had thought that part of her professional career was behind her, but recent events put the topic back to front and center of her work.

Terrlyn's daughters were both attending Griswold High School at the time. The foundation eventually approved Terrlyn and me to conduct the training; I would speak about the importance of narrative, sharing the stories of Rebeca, Mike, the Indian family, and the California couple, all people I met for this project. A major part of my focus was on real people with real stories. So instead of hiring a national consultant, Graustein was able to secure us as trainers when the collaborative turned to the very people who lived in this one square mile.

Alisha wasn't the only person I met through this project to join us for the conversation. Remember Josaphat Saint-Surin of Haiti and his son, Jonathan? Josaphat's wife, Kerline Barbot, and daughter, Thara, also took part in the training.

So did Phil Michel. I drove by the Wolverine Radio station on Main Street one night and saw through the window Phil talking with the radio host/owner. I had done a story on Phil and the issue of race came up in the interview. I really wanted his perspective, but he hadn't responded to my messages. So I pulled the truck over, ran inside, and teased him for making me track him down this way. On the spot, he happily agreed to participate.

When I did the story on him on a summer evening, Phil and his girlfriend at the time had ordered from Chopstix Chinese Restaurant on Main Street and were walking to Phil's house to watch a movie. They had seen *Deadpool* three or four times but were considering seeing it again.

Phil, seventeen, had graduated in June from Griswold High School and was headed to Three Rivers Community College in Norwich. He was undecided about a career goal, but was interested in art, writing, poetry, and working with youth.

Phil was living with his mother, Alisha, and her boyfriend on Mechanic Street. Phil and his mother moved to Jewett City from Uncasville when he was four. His brother, Ronel, fifteen, was living in Norwich with their father.

Though the brothers were separated by about ten miles, their cultural surroundings seemed even further apart. Phil's mother is white. Phil's father is Haitian. When Phil attempts Creole with Ronel, he gets light-heartedly teased in return for his limited vocabulary. "I live in a predominantly white community," Phil said. "I identify more with that. I don't match the stereotype of a black person."

In fact, when people ask Phil about his ethnicity, he tells them he's Sicilian, a running joke of his ever since watching the movie *The Godfather* and reading the book.

Phil's favorite memories of high school were of being a cast member of the musicals, a hugely popular event in town. He played comical roles until he took on a much more serious challenge as Judas in Jesus Christ Superstar that past spring. He also captivated audiences in school and other local venues with a passionate spoken word performance of Dr. King's "I Have a Dream" speech.

Readers' comments:

Beautiful story. You go, kids! Be great!

Phil, you are an awesome kid. You have a great attitude and will definitely go far.

Phil is an incredible musician that i have had the pleasure of watching for many years as he was im band with my son Curt i was in awe of his talent!

Rebeca Morales, the woman from Ecuador, had recently moved from Deep River to the borough to be a baker and manager of Giuliano's Bakery on Main Street. The bakery opened that April, filling the void left by the closure of the long-time popular Arremony's Bakery. Rebeca had been working at Giuliano's in Niantic for nearly a year.

In her younger years, Rebeca wanted to travel the world and one day become a doctor. She took another path with the birth of her son, Sebastian.

"Now I'm here," she said at the time, and then noted the irony. "In Jewett City, being a baker. In an Italian bakery."

Rebeca considered Jewett City to be a small, safe town that reminded her of the town she lived in Ecuador until she was eight. Her father left for the United States when she was four. He was given permanent residency at the time. Her son walked to and from school and said Griswold Public Schools had been welcoming.

My family bought Sebastian gifts for Christmas. She was so eager to return the favor, asking repeatedly how she could help my wife who had suffered with a kidney stone. But she abruptly packed up and moved back home to Florida to be with her ailing father and because she had lost the bakery job.

First, though, she joined us at our home for one of our cell groups. She texted me later to thank us and to say she had not felt the presence of God like she did during our meeting since when she first prayed to give her life to God.

I shared her story in the trainings on race.

The trainings turned out to be a highly inspirational time for the more than twenty of us who participated. Some shared personal, confidential stories of how racism affected their lives or how they began to realize their own hidden biases. When friends of mine heard I was helping conduct the training, they volunteered stories of their own. One of them, who is black, told me he deals with racism all the time. He remembered being on a construction job when one of the workers made loud, racist comments about Obama. My friend confronted him after several minutes and told him to stop. The man didn't listen. Eventually, the man who made the comments was fired. Luisa reminded me of another friend who had shared her story with us. She had been fired for allegedly stealing someone's ring at a nursing home. The woman was black. Another nurse also worked in the patient's room. She was white. The white woman was never questioned. And the ring was later found in his bed.

As part of our action plan, the group decided to host conversations about race in town. It's sorely needed.

Meanwhile, the Atlanta conference had a lasting impact on me. And so did the trip to the Civil Rights gallery, where, at the end of the tour, I visited the gift shop and came across a book stocked in the corner of the store that would deeply affect me. I read *A Gift of Love: Sermons from Strength to Love and Other Preachings* by Dr. King along with the eight trainings over four months, finding insight that helped me articulate a position on how to respond to what has been called the nation's unfinished agenda on race relations.

The Graustein training grant was followed by the foundation's offer to pay for a member to attend the Facing Race conference, which described itself as the nation's largest multiracial, intergenerational gathering for organizers, educators, creatives, and other leaders.

I'm still amazed to think I found myself standing in what once was the world's largest atrium at the Atlanta Marriott Marquis in that city's downtown. I'm not exactly comfortable with heights, so it took me a while to get used to the glass elevators that would shoot guests up through the center of the atrium. The conference was held in the adjoining hotel.

The project had launched me from the sidewalk just steps away from my front door to the center of the nation's racial justice movement where no one would have ever even considered our one square mile of the world. Yet I believe God had aligned the two movements—the hyperlocal one with the national one—in a way that enlarged my vision of how we can reach both the local community and the national stage at once. The world is in one square mile and the one square mile is in the world.

If the first part of this book is an encouragement to start the conversation, what this chapter should do is challenge us to see how we can guide that conversation and how we need to make sure that conversation addresses race.

Along the way in this project, I penned a prayer: Hidden hate is still hate. Bring it to light, Lord, and may the darkness flee, before it's too late. Hidden chains are still chains. Break them today, Lord. And may people walk free, before they forget they are indeed free. The wounds of injustice run deep, even to the next generation's very DNA. But Your love runs deeper, Jesus, even to the very soul and spirit. Bring freedom to unaware captives, Lord, and heal DNA pains.

Reflection and Actions Steps:

1. The California couple said that at the bar and on their walks downtown, people stare at them. A reader said the stares were likely due to the fact they were new faces in a small town. The reader imagined that they wouldn't get stares in a larger town. Which perspective do you lean toward? The visitors who say they feel unwelcome because of their race? Or the reader who says it's simply because they are new to the area? Why?
2. The man from India said he sees racism at the store he worked at. A reader gave him advice online: "Hang in there and smile. The good people will smile back and treat you decently. They're the ones that are worth getting to know anyhow." What advice would you have given?
3. Mike Mickens said that as a six-foot-two, three-hundred-pound African American," he suspected some people in his hometown are afraid of him. "They'd be surprised that I'm friendly." In Brooklyn, New York, he fit right in, he said. "I can be in a neighborhood full of Spanish, or full of Asians, or full of Caucasians. No matter where I am, I adapt." What does it mean to adapt to other races and cultures? Do you adapt to others? Is that positive or negative? What is your reaction to the fear Mike said others have about him?
4. Rebeca Morales described the racist community she first arrived in from Ecuador, where groups of students would push her to the ground and kick her. If someone like Rebecca arrived tomorrow in your hometown, how do you think they would be welcomed? Should any specific action be taken to ensure a safe, warm welcome? Who should take those steps?

Rebeca Morales with her son, Sebastian

Alisha Martin and her niece, Madison

THE WORLD IN ONE SQUARE MILE

Mike Mickens

Phil Michel

THE WORLD FOUND AMONG OUR IMMIGRANT NEIGHBORS

Lesson #6: "Take Notice and Speak Kindly" Is the Key to Immigrant Integration

Prior to launching this initiative, I approached the owner of a local business downtown and shared with him some basic premises behind the proposal. One of those premises was the idea that the world could be found in one square mile. By that, I largely meant the nations of the world, represented most often by new minority immigrants, were arriving in greater and greater numbers in our town. In another chapter, I show that there is more to that concept.

In any case, the owner didn't believe me. "I only see white people," he said of his customers and the people he sees on the streets as he drives to and from work. I tried to convince him he was wrong, but he would have none of it. He became an unofficial representative in my mind of the people who think this way—the people whose worlds have changed beneath their very noses and they haven't really paid attention.

I love sharing the stories of immigrants, whose lives inspire me. I wrote about the impact of immigration on Eastern Connecticut while working at the *Bulletin*, spending a year on one particular project that showed the amazing, historic transformation that was taking place in the region. Jobs at Mohegan Sun and Foxwoods Resort Casino drew a wave of immigration not seen since World War II. One key difference was that unlike the white Europeans who arrived in the 1950s, we witnessed immigrants of color from South and Central America, as well as Asia and Africa. Studies showed that immigrants were no longer just settling into the major cities of the United States, but were moving beyond those cities into less traditional destinations. Like Norwich. And Jewett City, a once nearly all white mill town.

I will never forget one day two years ago when I sat on the couch of our third floor, reading the book of Ruth in the Bible, a beautiful story which, as stories about immigrants often do, starts with a crisis.

This one started with a famine that forced a family of four to leave their homeland. Tragedy followed. Naomi's husband died. Ten years later, her two married sons died. When she heard the famine was over, she decided to go home. In an intensely emotional scene, she implored her daughters-in-law to stay behind. Remarry. Start over. She had nothing to offer them. They wept until one of the woman agreed. But Ruth clung to her, passionately responding that she would not let her go: "Don't ask me to leave you and turn back. Wherever you go, I will go; wherever you live, I will live. Your people will be my people, and your God will be my God. Wherever you die, I will die, and there I will be buried. May the Lord punish me severely if I allow anything but death to separate us!" (Ruth 1:16, 17 NLT).

It was sealed. Now it was Ruth's turn to live the life of a foreigner, an immigrant. So she put action into her words and went to work, picking grain in the fields. It was hard work. Long days. But she worked in the field of a just man. His name was Boaz, and he noticed right away there was someone new working in his massive fields. He asked about her. He was given a full report. He was deeply moved and so he called her over to talk. "Don't work in any other field," Boaz told her. "Work in mine, where it's safe. None of the men will harm you. And whenever you are thirsty you can drink." Stunned by his compassion she replied, "Why do you take notice of me. I'm a foreigner? "I've heard your story," he responds. "All of these kind words, they've comforted me," she answered (Ruth 2: 8–13 NLT).

It's that exchange between Boaz and Ruth that immediately leapt out to me in a way I had never read before. For all the complications surrounding the issue of immigration in the United States and around the world, the Bible spells out a simple, yet powerful call to action—take notice and speak kindly. Boaz took notice of Ruth. Asked about and heard her story, which created empathy within his heart. And then spoke kindly to her. It moved Ruth deeply. It made her feel welcome; made her feel like more than just an "other." And it became a sacred bond.

To take notice is to pay attention to someone and take sincere interest in the person's life. As you can see, being interested in people other than yourself—interested in their stories, their likes and dislikes, their trials and triumphs—rather than just our own self-interests is a major theme of this project.

As I have taken notice of the immigrants in Jewett City, I've made acquaintances with several families. There's a large, extended family of Ecuadorians who I came across years ago as they were playing volleyball in a dirt lot marked out in their backyard. I saw them again when our church was handing out Thanksgiving pies in their neighborhood and they were in the middle of cutting up a pig for a roast, its blood splashed across the concrete patio. When we stopped by one of the families' apartments to give them some clothes at Christmas, we stepped into the middle of a rehearsal in their living room of a song and dance they would later perform in front of families and friends for Christmas. They were dressed in traditional white and red outfits; Luisa and I considered it a privilege to be warmly welcomed into the lively atmosphere of a whole other culture. They invited us back for their holiday get-together at the local Veterans of Foreign War post. We accepted and were treated again to the food, music, and traditions of Ecuador just minutes from our home.

I got to later catch up with two of the family members in a spontaneous interview for this series.

I spotted a son, fourteen, walking with his mother on an errand first to the Jewett City Pharmacy and then, with shopping bags in hand, to JC's Uptown Laundromat. The Griswold eighth-grader planned to make dinner later at his apartment on Green Avenue.

"I make food for my family," he said. "It's our family culture to make rice and any kind of meat to go with it."

The son was born in New Jersey, but his parents were born in Ecuador. His parents left their native land for the United States for better education and economic opportunities for their children. The son has three older brothers and three older sisters. The mother said she misses home a lot. Homesickness plagues many immigrant families. She frequently calls her mother and has shared pictures with her son of the plot of land she owned in Ecuador that featured a big house, cows, sheep, and chickens. The family had been living in Jewett City for six years.

The son's twenty-three-year-old-brother lived with them at the time, along with the older brother's three-month-old daughter. The son said his niece was one of the best things that ever happened to him. "I get to take care of her," he said. He loves spending time with family. Several family members were living in two nearby apartments—one next to him and one behind him. His aunt was the one who encouraged his family to join her in Jewett City. All together, he said he has about forty family members living in Eastern Connecticut and Massachusetts.

"When we have parties, everyone gathers together, all our family members," he said. "It's kind of like a family reunion. It's us having fun and enjoying our lives."

The son said he believes his bilingual skills—he speaks English and Spanish—will help him one day in a career. At the same time, he was glad he could experience and enjoy American culture, such as barbecues. He wanted to become a professional soccer player; soccer is the most popular sport among his family and in Ecuador, he said. He said he looks up to his brother because he is a hard worker. On weekends, they spend time on PlayStation 4 together.

He was planning to visit family in Ecuador within a year for the first time.

Several times since this interview, I've noticed the son and his mother at Target shopping or as I drove by them while they were walking downtown. We wave to one another. And then one night, the son and his parents joined us for our cell group. Luisa held a conversation with them in Spanish, speaking kindly even as I shared with everyone present the gospel, which means good news. The son's face lit up when three others his age walked into the house, and he immediately recognized two of them from class.

Readers' responses:

Hi. I enjoyed learning more about you in this article. Thanks for being a peer helper the past few years. You're a fine young man and I wish you a successful year in grade 8 and beyond!

Any mother would be lucky to have you for a son! Good luck with your trip to Ecuador!!!

I've also enjoyed getting to know the extended Patel family, whom I first met for the stories I wrote on immigration for the *Norwich Bulletin* in 2006. In that year, twenty-six members of the family from India occupied three adjacent homes on Lenox Avenue. The white duplexes blended in with the rest of the neighborhood, but inside Anil Patel's home, the one in the middle, the culture of his native country remained alive—from the smell of spices simmering on the stove to the Hindu shrine in the grandparents' bedroom.

In fact, it helps me to understand that these spices simmer in several homes across Jewett City, an aroma that was almost completely foreign to the borough when I was growing up here.

At the time, Anil Patel told me the first in the family to arrive in the United States was his sister-in-law, Labhu, who was then living next door. She joined her family in New Jersey in the late 1980s. She returned to India to marry Anil's brother, came back, and applied for her parents to come. Anil followed in 1989, returning to India for an arranged marriage with Hansa. In the mid-1990s, Patel's parents became US citizens, inviting Patel's brother and sister to join the family. Eventually, Patel left his factory job in New Jersey and joined his family at a home in Preston as, one by one, the adults landed jobs at Foxwoods Resort Casino. The Patels bought two of the adjacent homes in Jewett City in 2000.

More than ten years after the in-depth series I wrote for the newspaper, I have watched as the Patel family has grown and intersected with my own family. One of the members is close friends to my youngest daughter and gave one of two speeches at their eighth-grade promotion. Anil left a crate of mangoes on my porch one day. We hosted him and another family member along with our family and friends for a celebration of the anniversary of Luisa's own arrival to the United States from Honduras.

For the One Square Mile series, Ratilal Patel immediately invited me inside when I spotted him while driving along Maple Street and I told him about the project. I had never visited him before, but he welcomed me and fed me.

Most Saturdays, members of the Patel family—as many as thirty-five at a time—get together for dinner at one of their homes in the borough on an unofficial rotating basis. They don't need a special occasion; they just enjoy one another's company. "We get together because in my country we live together—brothers, sisters, parents—not like here when kids get older and move away," Ratilal said.

Ratilal, sixty-three, was living with his wife, Lila, on Hill Street. But this afternoon, the gathering was on Maple Street. Ratilal was sponsored by his parents to move to the United States in 1977. He spent twenty-six years in Hoboken, New Jersey, before moving to Jewett City to join his family who had gradually moved here to work casino jobs. Ratilal worked at the former Wyre Wynd in town for two years. When we talked, he was employed at C&M Corp. in Dayville but was on disability following a knee replacement.

The happiest moment of his life was thirty-one years ago when Ratilal's twin son and daughter were born. The daughter was living in town, but the son was living in Stamford. They see the son often. "I provided him everything, and now he says, 'Forget about the work. Just come down here.'"

Readers' responses:
My neighbors! Very nice people

Very nice people!

Anima Patel shared One Square Mile's photo, December 13, 2015, Adam Bowles, this is a great thing you are doing for our little town. I've seen our town evolve so much through the years. Helping hands and welcoming and smiling faces on every corner even with the adversities people face. I guess that's what makes our town beautiful, and especially now with everything going on in today's world.

The Patels are also now my neighbors, with family members recently moving two houses away from mine. The Patel family wasn't around in Jewett City when I grew up. But I'm so glad they are here now.

India and Haiti are anecdotally the most represented new nationalities in the borough. I knew about the former. The latter somewhat surprised me. I was accustomed to the Haitian population that had grown in Greeneville, a section of nearby Norwich that is known as Little Haiti. But I had not realized how many were leaving Norwich for quiet towns and how many perceived Jewett City to be one of those quiet communities.

Faith is such a big part of their lives.

Jean Souvenance and Rose Meranvil's home on Aspinook Street still carried the aroma of dinner—beef and legume with white rice and black beans—even after their five children finished their meals on the night I drove by. Jeff, ten, and Noah, seven, played basketball outside; Colby, three, played on the Xbox downstairs; Carl, fifteen, spent time in his room; and Jasmine, five, played in and out of the house.

"Today has been good because I'm with my family and we've all been home together," said Jean, thirty-four and a chef at Windham Club in Windham. Rose's children were foremost on her mind, particularly with shootings that have taken place nationwide. "When they are not with me I feel very scared," said Rose, a certified nursing assistant who had planned to attend Goodwin College in Hartford the following semester to become a registered nurse. Both Jean and Rose are from Petit Goave, Haiti, a town that has seen an exodus of many of its residents to Eastern Connecticut. Rose moved to the United States more than twenty years ago because her mother, who had moved to this country when Rose was three, became a permanent resident and could invite immediate family. Jean moved to the United States more than fifteen years ago after his father, who was living in Norwich and working at Foxwoods Resort Casino, also became a permanent resident. His father has since returned to Haiti. The couple has lived on Aspinook Street for nine years.

One of the hardest situations Rose ever faced was more than two years ago when her aunt, Marie Delmas, died seven days after leaving Jewett City to return home to Haiti. She had been seemingly in good health while visiting with Rose and her family. Jean and Rose were attending Shekinah, a Seventh-day Adventist church in New London. She said her family prays together every day. Prayer, she said, is what keeps them together.

Readers' responses:

I recognize those kids. They always move to the side and wave when I drive by. Good kids.

A God centered praying family is a beautiful thing.

Beautiful family a joy to be able to teach their children nice to see them in the spot light like this

You have a beautiful family and your children have wonderful Manners. Thank you.

On one Saturday evening while my wife and I were driving through the borough, I met a fifteen-year-old international student from Shenzhen, China, which is what *Forbes* magazine once described as the second fastest-growing megacity in the world with a population of 12.51 million people. She was attending Norwich Free Academy and staying with a host family in town. On that evening she walked and then jogged to a gas station on North Main Street to get a gallon of whole milk. "It's quiet," she said of Jewett City. "I'm from a city. It's noisy. Many people. There's skyscrapers. Over here there's little houses."

She wanted to finish high school here and then attend university in the United States. Her parents had wanted her to study economics or business. She said she would rather study art. She said she doesn't miss home because she was able to connect with family via video calls and text messages. She discovered a taste for mozzarella here, but didn't like low-fat American food. "I have a happy life," she said.

Readers' responses:

Shenzhen is a rapidly growing city, i was there 3 times for a company i used to work for back between 1989 and 1991, was a lot of construction going on then, cant imagine what it looks like now, have pictures somewhere of it, it was a neat place to go

Good luck with your education. Hope you are having fun while you are here also. Thanks for sharing your story

I've been to Hong Kong and Taiwan with my grandfather to visit family, but I've never been to China. If I only went on what I read in the media, I'm sure my perspective would be skewed. After all, the Chinese are often portrayed only as our enemies. This student was here on a cultural exchange, but those exchanges don't always have to be formal. I simply noticed her, stopped, and talked to her.

As I drove through a nearby apartment complex, the same one where I ended up interviewing several people for this project, I spotted two people loading up furniture in a pickup truck. I stopped and learned this about them:

Newton Gomes moved to the United States from Cape Verde more than three years ago, spending most of the time since then living in Jewett City. In Cape Verde, Newton, thirty-three, supervised the distribution of confiscated items at a police station. But he moved here after his mother in Norwich petitioned for his permanent residency so he could seek better economic opportunities. His brother and sister were also living in Norwich.

In Cape Verde, Newton used to watch television and movies that depicted the United States in such a way that everything seemed larger than life. In fact, when he first went to McDonald's restaurant here he expected an even bigger hamburger than what he received. "Where's the other one?" he asked his mother, wondering if the smaller-than-expected hamburger meant he was getting two. Newton said he misses the food from home, especially the seafood. And he cried when he found out his best friend in Cape Verde died from an illness about three months prior to our talk. Newton was working in receiving and loading at Bob's Discount Furniture in Norwich.

That day, someone he knew in Cape Verde—but didn't become friends with until they met up in Norwich—helped him move from Mary Brown Apartments to a place in Preston. Newton wore a red tank top to match the red truck they used to move the belongings. Newton and his partner, Sierra Wirth, and their three young children needed more space. Newton met Sierra when she locked herself out of her car and he helped her. One day, he wants to own a home. For now, though, his American experience can be summed up by a cycle of "work, home, work" that kept him from getting to know people in the borough.

Many immigrants endure the same busy lifestyle, a reality that makes them long for their native homes. The cycle Newton described is what needs to be broken if immigrant integration is to succeed. He had not gotten to know any of his Jewett City neighbors because of an overly full work schedule, and now he was moving out of town.

One of the biggest challenges a man I met at the Jewett City Little League complex ever faced was learning English. He only knew Spanish when he first arrived in Norwich from Peru more than five years ago and it took him three tries—a test once every six months—before Three Rivers Community College in Norwich finally accepted him to take English classes. "The lady told me, 'I like your energy,'" said the forty-year-old man, who became a US citizen in 2016.

On this Friday afternoon, he and his wife took their three-year-old daughter to the park. The daughter collected stones and put them in a plastic bag to take home with her. He and his wife moved to an apartment on the south side of the borough more than two years ago, and said they prefer the quiet life here compared to Norwich, where the husband once lived. He last lived with his mother in nearby Oakdale. He moved to the United States when his mother sponsored his permanent residency. He said his family was all living in the United States, with several relatives living in Baltimore. The wife said she missed her father, mother, and brother back in Peru. The daughter was the wife's parents' only grandchild. The couple knew each other for many years but started dating when he went back to Peru for a vacation. They married about four years ago, and he went back and forth to visit her, but the absences depressed her and she moved here two years ago. It was an expensive move that the husband had to save for. His goal was to be a policeman. He once was a chef at a restaurant in Lima, the capital of Peru, where he said the food is among the best in the world. He was working as a dealer at Mohegan Sun casino.

I met the family that lives in my old house just around the corner from me for this project. We had sold that home to our friends, Noah and Stephanie White, but, after nearly ten years of living on Faust Street, they moved to another house in town. It was strange to return to my old house where both our girls were little and not know the family that lives there. But life goes on. And in this case, the latest family to live there seemed to once again signal the ethnic and cultural shift of our neighborhood.

John Clemens was one of the family members living in the house, and we struck up a conversation on his back deck. The deck was built after we moved, but the yard brought back memories, including one of Tori speeding in her Barbie jeep with Roni in the passenger seat. Roni's little hands were raised in the air, and her face beamed with excitement in the photo we have of that moment. When Roni was just seven years old, she told me one night she couldn't sleep because she was trying to dream amazing dreams on purpose. On her fifteenth birthday, I told her to keep dreaming amazing dreams on purpose and to always remember we serve an amazing, dream-giving God. Both Tori and Roni are among the biggest inspirations in my life, and this house was home to so many memories of them both as little ones.

John's father and mother separated when he was seven after years of a turbulent relationship. At age twenty-two, John still didn't have any contact with his father, but that void left him with a dream to go to college and become a social worker.

"I didn't have a father so, like with orphans, I want to help them, and street kids," he said.

John had recently moved with his mother, Concep Ramirez, his sister, Rio Ramirez, his sister's boyfriend, Raffy Alcala, and his nephew and niece to the home Rio bought on Faust Street. They had been living in an apartment in Plainfield, where John graduated high school in 2013 and where he lived for nine years. His nephew, Ace, was ten at the time. His niece, Coleen, was two.

Coleen is the first in the family to be born in the United States. The rest of the household was born and raised in the Philippines. John was twelve when his family left the Philippines to reunite with family living in New Jersey.

"I was a little nervous to be in school because I didn't understand English," he said. "I was like an outcast. After one year, I got used to it."

John ended up in Eastern Connecticut because his aunt and her husband moved from New Jersey to the area after landing jobs at Foxwoods Resort Casino. He described Jewett City as "quiet and nice." "I like what I see," he said. "I like Main Street."

His family speaks Filipino at home. His favorite childhood memories are of meeting and making friends with other street children in the Philippines. He said his mother sold clothing on the streets and was rarely home. So while she was out, he would play basketball or swim with the other children, forming a family-like bond.

John had two aunts who were living in Plainfield; one in Thompson; and another, Reivaj Javier, in California.

"I'm just satisfied with what I have," he said, before driving to his aunt's house in Plainfield. "I have my family. If I didn't have them, I'd be sad."

John said he wants to be a father figure to others. He defined a good father as someone who provides loving discipline and encourages without criticizing.

John enjoyed playing the bass and listening to rock music. That night, he planned to join cousins and watch the New England Patriots on TV.

So to the business owner who only sees Jewett City as what it was a decade ago, or even five years ago, here's the nations I discovered represented in this tiny borough: Cape Verde, Peru, China, Haiti, Ecuador, India, and the Philippines. I also wrote about someone from Guatemala and three brothers from El Salvador. And, as I showed in the final story of the series with my wife as the subject, Honduras. There's one more. Luisa's story elicited this response from Rosh Shekarestan Disch, a reader who happened to become the subject of one of the profiles:

"Wonderful! Your wife (and you) are an inspiration to us all! I feel lucky to have met you that day at the Little League field! You can add Shiraz, Iran to your list of where people from your stories were born! I was born in that far away world and brought here when I was a little over a year old on the last flight to leave that country commercially for almost a decade. One day later and I would not be here today."

I was intrigued and months later asked Rosh for a more detailed account. She returned the Facebook message just an hour later with the following story:

"I was born in Shiraz, Iran, in January of 1977. Back then, Iran, led by the Shah Reza Pahlavi, was well on its way to becoming one of the most progressive and cosmopolitan countries of the world. My parents were very happy living in Iran, but both came from large families (8 siblings on each side) and they recognized the best way to support themselves and the lifestyle they wanted to provide my older sister and me was to get a higher education in America, where they believed opportunity knocked at every corner.

"Before I turned 2, my father made this dream a reality by trekking to the United States to stay with a friend in Oklahoma and to set up a place for my mom and sister and me to live while he studied at university. Oklahoma was not one of the states he had been accepted to college in, but having a friend nearby in a foreign land is priceless and so my dad decided to make Oklahoma our home for the next 4 years little did he know he would be living there still almost 40 years later.

"A few months after he got settled, my father sent for my mom, sister and me. At the time, flights departing Iran overseas usually departed in the middle of the night (2–3am). My mom, left on her own in Iran, was running late and we missed our flight. We were forced to wait until the next night to take off. My mom says she'll never forget I was being carried by my paternal grandfather whom I had a particular bond with. She said right before we boarded the flight, he held me close, told me he loved me, to be well and said he knew he would never see me again. My mom thought that to be odd since we would only be gone for 4 years and back in time to start school.

"Our plane took off and we began the next big journey. This was December of 1978. That flight we were on out of Iran became the LAST commercial flight to leave Iran for the U.S. for the next 8 years. Soon afterwards, the Shah fled Iran and the Iranian Revolution occurred. Immediately thereafter we had Iran Contra and then the devastating Iran-Iraq war.

"The years kept going and our lives in America became solidified. Before we new it, my dad graduated from business school and we entered the school system in America and made a life for ourselves. It was incredibly unsafe back in Iran and by the time we could realistically travel back my sister and I didn't know how to read or write the language, we were both almost done with elementary school, my brother was born and was a U.S. citizen, and we had grown roots here. When I was in the 3rd grade, my paternal grandfather died of colon cancer in Iran. It was 6 years after he had said goodbye to me. He knew even then what none of us ever dreamed. We would not be back. As a matter of fact, the next time any of us went to Iran for a visit, I was 17 years old and it was the summer before my senior year in high school. It was a bittersweet trip. My parents went back expecting the cosmopolitan country they left behind. Instead they saw a war-torn place so regimented with rules and lacking the freedoms they had become accustomed to. I went, excited to meet so many cousins and aunts and uncles I grew up not knowing. Remember, there was no Facebook or iPhones back then. Anything I knew about my family back in Iran was from translated letters written in Farsi and the handful of pictures that accompanied them. I spent 7 weeks that summer in Iran. That was 23 years ago. I've never been back and I wonder what I would have done differently, things I might have said to family members, had I known I never would be back.

"I should mention, my parents both became naturalized U.S. citizens when I was in 5th grade. My sister and I filed paperwork at the same time but had to wait until we were 18 to formally change our citizenship. The age of consent."

That's at least eleven nations represented by first-generation immigrants I met in this one square mile. After discovering so many people from different ethnic backgrounds, I wonder how much stronger our communities would be if more of us simply and deliberately took notice of our immigrant neighbors and their stories and went out of our way to speak kindly to them. A few welcoming words would go a long way. We are missing out! The convergence of cultures in our communities is an historic opportunity. We can learn about the world around us. And we can learn this right in our own square miles.

Yet, the Billy Graham Center says less than one in ten immigrants has even been invited into the home of an American. I am convinced the revival of spiritually dead, culturally insensitive, and racially hostile hearts won't just happen in church seats, but at dinner tables and on front porches in homes across the nation.

CNN reported on March 26, 2017, that Senators Tim Scott of South Carolina and James Lankford of Oklahoma launched "Solution Sundays," in which people are encouraged to invite a family of another race over to your home for a meal on Sunday. Many new immigrants are of another race, I would add. Senate Chaplain Barry Black told CNN he grew up in Baltimore and didn't shake hands with a white person until he was sixteen years old.

"Now how does that happen in the United States of America? But we never invited someone who didn't look like us home for dinner either," said Black, as quoted in the story by Abigail Crutchfield, Dana Bash, and Jeremy Harlan.

Matthew Soerens, the US church training specialist for World Relief whom I have grown to admire from a distance as he speaks out on behalf of immigrants, wrote a Facebook post mostly based on the first chapter of Exodus that caught my attention. He gave me permission to use it here.

Pharoah "quietly asks Joseph to identify the most skilled shepherds from among his brothers to take charge of his own sheep, and he seeks the blessing of the patriarch Jacob (Genesis 47:5–6, 10). As theologian Justo Gonzalez has observed, Pharoah recognized that an immigrant like Joseph could present a significant opportunity to the nation that received him, and he thus responded with hospitality.

Matthew wrote that "In the book of Exodus, though, we find a starkly different response to immigrants. He quoted Exodus 1:8 (NLT): "Eventually, a new king came to owner in Egypt who knew nothing about Joseph or what he had done." Matthew continued: "Without the context of a personal relationship, this Pharoah saw the significant numbers of Joseph's descendants, and he considered them a threat to his nation's national security. He didn't want to deport the Israelites because he benefits economically from their labor, but he is unwilling to grant them the same rights as native-born Egyptians. Eventually, Pharoah's fear so escalates that he takes dramatic action, decreeing the genocide of all newborn Hebrew boys. His response to these foreigners is seeing a threat and responding with hostility."

The immigrant conversation in America needs the context of personal relationship.

The ethnic makeup of the neighborhood I live in has changed dramatically in ten years. I now have Chinese neighbors across the street and Indian neighbors two houses down from me and Filipino neighbors around the corner. Relationships across cultures don't happen overnight. But you have to start somewhere, so why not with where you live? With a little time and patience, hospitality will overcome hostility.

"We are here for only a moment, visitors and strangers in the land as our ancestors were before us. Our days on earth are like a passing shadow, gone so soon without a trace," says the New Living Translation of 1 Chronicles 29:15. Other translations say we are all foreigners. From God's perspective, we are all immigrants passing through this life in this temporary home He called Earth and that He created for us. Whatever the policies that need to be debated and created, let's at least start with what a friend of mine says is our "shared humanity."

Reflection and Action Steps:

1. How many nations are represented in your one square mile?
2. Invite an immigrant neighbor to dinner. Tell him or her you want to hear his or her story.
3. Host an international potluck in your school or church.
4. Train immigrant leaders to host families across the community in their homes or at events to share their own stories in their own words—"living museum" style.

Jean Souvenance and Rose Meranvil and their children

Newton Gomes, left, and his friend

John Clemens

Ratilal Patel, center, and his family

THE WORLD OF BIG STORIES IN SMALL TOWNS

Lesson #7: To Expand Your Vision, Break Your World Down to One Square Mile

No matter how big your city is, you can always break it down to life in one square mile—or at least the spirit of that concept, if your one square mile happens to be relatively isolated. As a matter of fact, the larger the territory, the more a person can feel lost, disconnected. First, reduce your world to your neighbors. Listen. Pay attention. Then watch as your vision expands even as the focus narrows.

I cherish small-town life, or one-square-mile life, more than ever after getting to meet more people than ever in my hometown. I love drives through the borough of Jewett City. I see neighbors who I wave at, take in familiar views of the park that sparkle with natural beauty, roll past community pillars such as banks, pharmacies, the florist, the Little League field, the library.

The values of friendship and family and way of life—a slower pace—in small towns have much to offer to communities nationwide and can be captured and celebrated in even densely populated square miles.

It takes focus on what matters. It takes appreciation for the things that money can't buy. It takes slow walks around the block. Hellos to your neighbors. Pauses. Willingness to be interrupted.

The following vignettes speak for themselves and attest to these values. I trust they will endear you to life in this borough and open your eyes to life in your corner of the world.

When Life Mirrors a Country Song

A country song came on the radio the June day I met Dayle Lewis outside her home that made her cry. She couldn't remember the title, but the lyrics talked about a couple that had been married for fifty-eight years despite skeptics who said they'd never make it.

"It made me think of my mom and dad," Dayle said, wiping away tears once again.

Her father died four years ago. Her mother, Cora Merritt, ninety-one, later moved in with Dayle. Her parents had been married sixty-eight years despite a relative saying they'd never last.

Dayle's mother was suffering dementia. But she enjoyed sitting on a rocking chair on Dayle's porch—which she was doing that night—listening to the birds, watching the squirrels, and spending time with her family.

Dayle welcomed a visit from a longtime friend, Janice Longton, a neighbor on Mathewson Street. Janice held Freckles, her fourteen-year-old Daschund, as the two talked about the fish in Dayle's outdoor pond and Fourth of July plans.

Dayle had lived in her home for thirty years. "I said I'd never live here," she said of Jewett City. But her husband, Jim, liked the house because it reminded him of the one he lived in while in Virginia.

Janice moved from Norwich to her home on Mathewson Street more than thirteen years ago. Her two grown children were living side-by-side in a duplex also on Mathewson Street. As Janice shared the story of her arrival in Jewett City, Jim walked by and pointed at her, joking, "She just got her ankle bracelet off. We all did. That's why we're here."

Dayle and Janice worked near each other—Dayle as a hairdresser for forty years at East Lyme and Janice as the director of environmental services for Essex Meadows, a senior retirement community in Essex. Their proximity as neighbors and as workers has helped foster their years-long friendship, they both said.

Thanks to readers' reactions to this story and confirmation from

Dayle, the song in question turned out to be "Love Like Crazy," by Lee Brice.

Readers' responses:

Thanks for sharing this. I live around the corner and love seeing the ever changing front yard holiday displays. It's nice to know a little about your neighbors even if you don't talk much.

Shelly Martinez: It's good to see the neighbors caring about each other.

Shelly Martinez is a cohost of a local country music radio show, WCTY.

As a postscript, I visited Janice at her home to get permission to use her name in this book. She told me she was moving to a trailer home in Canterbury. The reason? Freckles died, she told me in tears. "I need to get out of this place," she said. In fact, Dayle didn't even know yet she was moving. They had seen less of each other because Janice no longer walked by Dayle's home, which she used to do with her dog.

Friday Night Lights

Dakota Pedro, eighteen, had a car but decided to walk from his home on Tift Street to Dean's Corner Diner for breakfast the Saturday morning I saw him.

"I was just thinking of growing up here," he said on his walk home along Route 12. "I can't even imagine how many times I've gone up and down these sidewalks. These streets feel like home. When I'm older and leave this town, I'll always come back and drive through and reminisce about so many different things."

Dakota was living with his mother, Jackie Tetreault, and his twin brother, Dylan. Dakota is a 2015 Griswold High School graduate. He played football all four years, including middle linebacker as a senior.

He cried tears of joy when Griswold upset Norwich Free Academy in the regular season.

"Everyone who has grown up playing Griswold football always says they miss it," Dakota said. "Just playing on the field with your friends and brothers. Friday night lights—you can't really beat that."

Dakota was working as a flagger for Norwich Public Utilities and was headed into his second year at Three Rivers Community College in Norwich. He was still unsure of a career goal. He said one of his greatest strengths is perseverance. "I never give up," he said.

The way Dakota talked about missing being on a team stayed with me. I invited him to our cell group and was pleasantly surprised when he took me up on my offer. He has been twice now. He then came to a Christmas service. And then he came to my brother-in-law's house to watch a football game with a few of the guys. And now we keep in touch. All from a spontaneous conversation.

Readers' responses:

Good job Dakota, I am so proud of you. Life is full of many different paths. Always let the Lord lead you as to which ones to take and you'll go far and be truly happy

No Time for Self-Pity

Bill Couture grew up in a home on Faust Street until age eighteen, where he remembered camping in the backyard and chasing his sister. Bill, sixty-five, had moved from Moosup back into the house four years ago after his stepmother died. His mother and father had died previously.

"I've come full circle," he said as he watered his garden right after he mowed the lawn. He was preparing for "Bill's Fall Ball," or the hosting of family at his house that Saturday to celebrate several special occasions, including his daughter's thirtieth birthday, which was the day of our interview. Bill's girlfriend, Sherry Burns, had recently turned fifty-five.

Bill's son, Bill, was working as the assistant vice president of business loans at Jewett City Savings Bank. He was married to Kim. Bill's daughter, Desirae, was married to Jason Violette. Their son,

Landon, was two at the time. Desirae, an occupational therapist, was pregnant with their second son.

Bill was a Teamster truck driver for ABF Freight in Plainfield for twenty-two years but retired after suffering a motorcycle accident seven years ago that month. A woman pulled her vehicle out in front of him as he was riding along Sheldon Road. His foot was injured so badly in the accident he had to have it amputated. He has a camouflage prosthetic. "You can't see it, right?" he said, laughing.

Bill said he still rides a three-wheeled motorcycle.

"The way I look at it you can either go into a corner and say, 'Poor, poor, pitiful me,' and don't do anything," he said. "Or when you fall you can get right back up."

Readers' comments:

Aloha Bill I remember you and Jay Hlastava had a place on East Main Street you guys introduced me to tacos for the first time I think I ate more than half a dozen good to see you again.

Good man, with a great attitude and awesome son.

Inspiring!!

The Best of Both Worlds

I stopped Rosh Disch as she was walking from the baseball field at Jewett City Little League to the picnic tables across the parking lot. I learned her career began in Los Angeles, one of the great cities of the world, and yet she was settled here with her family and thriving in small-town life.

She told me she landed a job with the Wedding Channel after graduating from UCLA in 2000. Rosh had high expectations of where her career as a writer in Los Angeles would take her. But it didn't exactly start off as she had dreamed.

"Have you seen *The Devil Wears Prada?*" she said, referring to a movie about a recent college graduate who becomes the assistant to a demanding editor-in-chief at a prestigious magazine. "Well, that was my life. I was an errand girl. They even called me Cookie."

Rosh gave three weeks' notice of her resignation, but someone from human resources stepped in and discovered the problem was not with Rosh but with her boss. The CEO then walked with Rosh downtown, explained there would no longer be a problem, and urged her to stay and learn any aspect of the company she wanted. Eventually, she became the producer of Couture, New York's Bridal Fashion Week's premiere luxury trade show. The Wedding Channel is now owned by The Knot.

Along the way in her bicoastal existence, she met Ellis Disch while he was in law school in Boston College. She and Ellis, a 1996 Norwich Free Academy graduate, married in 2005. After the birth of their first child, Emma-Kate, then ten, they paused to consider their future. He left his position at a national law firm so they could move back to his hometown and spend more time with his family. Rosh's father-in-law, Peter Disch, was the owner of Disch Motor Group. Ellis operated Thrifty Car Sales in North Franklin with his family.

"They have such warmth, honesty, and integrity," said Rosh, a theater major and actress since age three. "I'm just so proud to be part of the family."

Rosh and Ellis had three children at the time. Rosh said she loves being a mother. Like she does with anything she is committed to, she said, "you throw yourself into it with abundant vigor." She said she is the type to bake reindeer cupcakes for the class and text the photos to her friends, one of whom joked and texted back the napkins she brought to her child's classroom.

The couple moved from Norwich to Griswold in 2011 after they found a home on three acres next to two farms. Her children were enrolled in a charter school in Norwich.

"I was afraid to leave what I thought was a good thing, but it wasn't until we moved to the Griswold school system that they really blossomed," Rosh said.

Rosh said she enjoyed country life as well as the proximity to Boston and New York. "It's the best of both worlds," said Rosh, who grew up in Oklahoma. That day, Emma-Kate had her first sleepover at a friend's house. And Rosh took Oliver, then eight, and Lily, then six, to the Jewett City Little League complex, where they waited for the rest of Oliver's all-star teammates to show up. Lily, dressed in a fairy outfit, was upset by some children at the playground who she said laughed at her. At Rosh's request, Oliver stopped what he was doing to walk with her to the park, putting his arm around her and promising to protect her.

The last time Rosh cried was nearly two months earlier on July 24, as she remembered her sister, Buffy, who died at age thirty-three of colon cancer on the same date in 2008. Rosh was the chief operating officer and site director of an international online wedding planning resource site, which was due to debut the following week.

Readers' comments:

That mom who just brought the napkins she's brilliant.

Awe Lily ❤ *Your outfit is beautiful… just like you are!!! Rosh Shekarestan Disch xox*

Soooooo well done!!! Fabulous piece and what a Beautiful Family in more ways than one!!!!!

Friends for Life

People say big cities are plagued with loneliness despite the crowds. In my small town, I have discovered amazing friendships. But these friendships take time—sometimes years.

Deb Bingell and Pat Stott's friendship spanned fifty years when we met, a connection rooted in the borough and the town where their lives have so often intersected.

Pat, who worked at the former Wyre Wynd in Jewett City for thirty years, was working as an accountant's assistant for an office in Pawcatuck. Deb was working as a bookkeeper for the Jewett City Department of Public Utilities, where she had worked for nearly thirty-three years.

Their friendship began in the third grade.

"We were in the same class and we clicked," Deb said as the two paused from their evening walk. "On the same token, our families knew one another. My father was in her parents' wedding. He was an usher. And her father was in my parents' wedding. And (Pat) was in my wedding. And I was in her wedding."

Deb and Pat graduated from Griswold High School in 1975.

"We took every single class in high school together," Pat said. "Except in our senior year we ended up in different home rooms. That's the only time we were separated."

Deb, who had two grown children, was living in the Pachaug section of town. Pat, who had been married to John for thirty-five years, was living in the borough. They walked together three to four times a week. "We catch up on the gossip," Pat said, laughing. "We vent," Deb added.

Pat teared up as she described a recent demonstration of the depth of their friendship. Her mother died on Christmas in 2012. Deb often went with Pat to visit Pat's mother in the convalescent home prior to the death, and after the mother died Pat spent a lot of time talking about the loss with Deb.

Pat offered a definition of friendship: "Someone who's there for you. Not only in the good times, but especially in the bad times."

Readers' comments:

Leona Sharkey (also profiled for this project): Great story and two wonderful women!

Renee Assmar: Heartwarming testimony to genuine friendship. Enjoyable piece, Adam Bowles!

Jewett City Pride!! Friends!!

Love these heartwarming stories about my hometown! Keep them coming.

All in the Family

I interviewed Brianna Wilson on her break from her job at Charlene's Diner on a Tuesday afternoon as she went for a walk past my house with her seven-year-old nephew, Brayden Marquis, and her dog, Max.

Brayden, who had his own broom for chores at the diner, was wearing the jersey of his favorite NBA player—Steph Curry of the Golden State Warriors. Max, a Golden Retriever, was eight months old.

Brianna, meanwhile, said she was still on cloud nine after getting engaged the week before to Brandon Kudelchuk.

Brianna said she took pride in being a part of a family business on Main Street. Her grandmother, Charlene Schultz, has operated the diner since 1979. Brianna's mother, Susie Langlois, was helping to run it, and Brianna's sister, Brittany Marquis, was working there as well.

Wally Lamb, a local best-selling author who shot to fame when his book *She's Come Undone*, was selected for Oprah's Book Club, visited the diner in 2014 for the filming of a scene of the movie adaptation of his novella *Wishin' and Hopin'*. The diner was considered an ideal location for a film set in Christmas 1964.

Brianna realized how much she appreciated the work at the diner after one year as a student at Central Connecticut State University in New Britain in 2010. She did not enjoy the social atmosphere of the campus and did not return.

"I had an identity crisis almost," she said. "I know New Britain is not that big, and some students go across the country. Maybe I'm being dramatic, but I'm small town and very close to my family."

Where Everyone Knows Your Name

Dominic Scavoini, who I used to attend high school with in town, felt the same way as Brianna.

The view from the home he was renting on Carley Avenue features Ashland Lake, Veterans Park, and the French Club. In other words, Dominic said on the Saturday I interviewed him, it's iconic in a Norman Rockwell kind of way.

"People live their whole lives wanting to live on the water," Dominic said he tells his children. "But for this moment, this time, we have this." This also included a slice of beachfront, water-skiers who occasionally made waves as they sped by, and Pumpkinseed sunfish.

Dominic and his wife, Chrissy, a licensed practical nurse, had five children in a blended family. His then thirteen-year-old son, John, from a previous marriage recently called Chrissy Mom a few times. "I tried that to see how it felt," said John, an avid reader.

Dominic, who turned forty-three that Monday, had lived in town since the fourth grade, minus a brief time away. He was a coadministrator of a Facebook page called "You are probably from Jewett City/Griswold if." It had 2,050 members.

Rebecca Phelps started the page, but Dominic asked to help operate it.

"People were making a lot of derogatory comments, and it needed cleaning up," he said. "I asked her to make me a coadministrator because it needed some babysitting."

Dominic, who was working at Ed's Garage in Canterbury, particularly loved posts of old photos of the borough. He was attracted to the small-town atmosphere of Jewett City. One of his children even asked if he was famous because "everywhere we go someone knows you."

"You aren't going to get me out of Jewett City," Dominic said. "It's home."

Readers' comments:

Thank you. God bless ALL of you. Growing up here is truly comfort.

Awesome story, will be glad to share this book with my grandkids one day and say, yep this guy right here helped build that crazy maze!

I live on Carley avenue for years.our backyard had the same view. cant remember the number, but third house on left.

Celebrating 80s Hair in a Modern World

I bumped into another high school classmate for one of my interviews. In my senior yearbook, Jo-Ann Flynn said we'd be friends forever. Of course, as so often is the case, we went our separate ways. Still, she and I never left our hometowns. Several others I know haven't either. And it's not because they are stuck here, although I acknowledge some people seem afraid to ever leave their one square mile.

During Griswold High School's production of the musical *9 to 5* a few years ago, there was a need for someone to do the hair of the cast members in the style of the 1980s. So they called on one of the parents—Jo-Ann.

"They said my hair looked like the 80s," she said that Saturday, laughing.

Jo-Ann has helped with hair and make up for Griswold's plays ever since. She was purchasing three bouquets at the Jewett City Greenhouse for students she had helped the last few months in preparing for *Jesus Christ Superstar*, a musical playing at the school that week.

"It's the best show in years," she said. "I don't even have a kid on the stage."

Jo-Ann and her husband, Zachary Flynn, were living on Popple Bridge Road in Griswold. They had two children at the time: Kiley, who planned to come home the following week after completing her freshman year at Boston College, and Kieran, who was a freshman at Griswold.

The hardest moment of Jo-Ann's life was when she learned that Kiley had Type 1 diabetes when Kiley was ten. Jo-Ann found out at 8:00 a.m. and four hours later was already administrating insulin shots. Kiley was confused and wondered if she had done something wrong. Jo-Ann had to encourage her to be strong while at the same time she herself would break down in tears.

"You think you have really healthy children," said Jo-Ann, who was working as the director of Futures Inc., which provides services for individuals with disabilities. "But it can happen to anybody."

Readers' comments:

Blessed to have her and her family in our lives.

She's just as beautiful as I remember her in school!! Nice to hear these stories!

You do so much more for Griswold on top of the drama, thanks for all you do! We appreciate it! See you at soccer!

Zachary Flynn: Nice article to nice to be my spouse?

It Takes a Village

Leona Sharkey, like Jo-Ann Flynn, is another fellow 1991 GHS graduate. She lived a street away from me. Tim Sharkey, her husband, had lived his entire life on Lenox Avenue, where they resided next door to his childhood home. I didn't know that about him. I scheduled their interview.

The stories Tim shared about life in the neighborhood were told with laughter and nostalgia.

"That was the yard," Tim said, giving the word *the* extra emphasis. He referred to a fenced-in section belonging to Norman Gileau, retired principal from Griswold High School and the subject of a profile I referred to in the chapter on the wisdom of seniors. "We played football, basketball, soccer, hide-n-seek, tag."

"Everybody's parents took care of everybody's children," he said earlier that week from the kitchen of his home.

When the Gileaus went on family trips to Misquamicut Beach in Rhode Island or Rocky Neck State Park in Niantic, they invited the neighborhood children to join them in their station wagon. Tim, who is the youngest of six siblings, said his family had little money, so he especially appreciated those outdoor ventures.

Tim, who was serving as an elected borough burgess, and Leona, who was working as a tax collector and secretary for Jewett City, had lived in their home since 1997. The previous owners were Mr.

and Mrs. Peters, his German-speaking neighbors. Tim's father was a World War II veteran. Mr. Peters fought for the Germans. "He was a Nazi," Tim said. But his father, Herbert, and Mr. Peters got along great, playing cards and drinking into the night. Tim remembered as a boy overhearing his father joking with Mr. Peters. His father teased he once had Mr. Peters in his crosshairs but lowered his gun—a fable. "He said, 'I wasn't going to shoot him. He's a good German,'" Tim recalled. "Mr. Peters just laughed." The Peters were generous with Tim and his family, and he fondly remembers getting "real German chocolate with real alcohol in it" at Christmas.

So when the house went for sale, Tim acted. "I couldn't let this go," he said.

Tim and Leona had been married for nineteen years and together for twenty-three when we talked in their kitchen. She was just nineteen when Tim first saw her at the Jewett City Pizza Palace. "She had long, beautiful hair. She was wearing a comedy and tragedy brooch. I thought, 'I've got to meet her.'" His friend Bob Hanson, chief of the A. A. Young Jr. Hose & Ladder Co., introduced him. Leona was close friends with Georgia LaBonne, whose family runs the restaurant. Both families remain close.

Tim and Leona have a son, Logan, who soon after graduated from Norwich Technical High School. "Besides my wife, he's the best thing that ever happened to me," Tim said. Logan's birth prompted Tim to resign after twenty-one years from the fire department, where he had risen to deputy chief and was a first responder to the March 12, 1995, arson that destroyed the Ashland Mill, now Veterans Memorial Park. After responding to two separate fatal accidents and returning to his newborn son, Tim decided he wanted to give up his career to be with his family.

Perhaps the worst thing to happen to Tim was a motorcycle accident he suffered in 1991 on Route 12 near Green Onion restaurant. "I died twice," he said. During his recovery, he felt this near-uncontrollable urge to thank everyone he saw. One day his sister, Patty Stone, took him on an errand to the bank. On the way home, she took him to St. Mary's Church, lit some candles, told him to take his time and that she'd be waiting in the back. "When I walked out the door—and I'm not a religious person—(the burden) was gone. I made my peace."

He described in detail the out-of-body experience he had following his accident. "I saw this light. It wasn't yellow. It was snow white. If you look up at the sun it hurts your eyes but it didn't hurt your eyes. There was a grassy hill. As I walked up I was welcomed by people on either side, like in a parade. I saw my grandmother halfway up the hill. We had a conversation. I wanted to stay but she said, 'It's not your time.'"

Doctors dubbed him the miracle man. And if he's the miracle man, Tim called Leona his angel for coming into his life at the right time soon after.

Readers' comments:

What a beautiful love story!

Love it!! What an amazing journey! So glad to have been a part of your lives my friends!!

You learned a wonderful life lesson from your father and Mr. Peters.

I SO remember the beginning of your relationship together. You were so cute about Leona! ❤❤❤

You couldn't have picked and or stumbled on to a better "Interviewee" in my opinion. Tim "Is" Jewett City and Mr. Gileau's yard was the corner stone of Tim's neighborhood. We all had our own neighborhood to hang in I guess is the word, ya know ride bikes, play kickball be kid's and do what kid's do however Tim's neighborhood certainly took that to a new level Mr. Gileau's yard was the envy in my younger self! Best Interview Yet!

A Town with Lifelong Residents

Perhaps few local personalities are as recognizable as Al Geer. His then cohost on local Wolverine Radio dubbed him "Mr. Jewett City." It's a fitting nickname when you consider Al was a seventy-year-old, life-long resident in town, with more than 30 years spent in a home he rented on Hill Street in the borough.

His Jewett City experience was varied: a member of the last class to graduate from Riverside Grammar School in 1963; time living in an apartment above the former Arremony's bakery and waking up to the aroma of freshly baked pastries; thirty years in the A. A. Young Jr. Hose & Ladder Co. where he worked his way up to lieutenant in the rescue division; political service as a burgess for a couple of terms and as the warden for one term; and a part-time police officer with the former Jewett City police department.

In recent days, new experiences weighed on his heart. That morning he was still grumbling good-naturedly about his beloved Boston Red Sox and what he said was poor umpiring the night before in a loss against the New York Yankees.

When he walks upstairs at home, Al said he begrudgingly admits his children might be right about the wisdom in moving to a one-level home to make it easier on his aging body.

And his wife of forty years, Donna, died of a heart attack on February 4, 2015, a loss he was still grieving. Donna, who once drove a school bus in town, was a child and with her father when he died of a heart attack while delivering propane as part of a job he had in Windham.

In the early days of his grief, Al met Mike Minarsky—the subject of a profile referred to in the chapter about extraordinary people—who lived nearby and who was launching a local radio program. Al had trouble sleeping and ended up visiting Mike's home at 3:00 a.m. some mornings to help record segments of the show.

Of course, Al had a life outside the borough, including a three-year administrative stint in the US Army, and a twenty-two-year career in security with the criminally insane for the state of Connecticut, first at the Norwich Hospital in Preston and then Whiting Forensic Institute in Middletown. He once won a scratch-off lottery that provided him and his wife an all-expenses paid trip to Las Vegas, where he went on to win another $34,000. And he used to take wedding photos and worked as a DJ for parties. He considered writing an autobiography called *Full Circle*, because he went from working as a judicial marshal at Norwich Superior Court to bail bondsman. He said criminals liked him better when he released them and not when he arrested them.

Al said despite all his local credentials he was most proud of his marriage, two children—Michelle Chaffee, and his son, Frank Geer, a Norwich resident and full-time firefighter for Mohegan Sun casino—and four grandchildren.

Al said he and his wife would have brief, uncomfortable conversations about what would happen in the event one of them died. But he recommended people have honest discussions about death. "Nobody wants to die, but you do die," he said matter-of-factly. He said he believes in life after death and that heaven awaits him. "I accepted Jesus as my savior in my early years as a teenager when I went to Calvary Chapel in Canterbury."

Readers' comments:

Al gave me a warning once for headbanging and playing the drums while driving. Thnx Officer Geer :)

Wow—didn't know they lived above Arremony's bakery. Such a nice story!

(Al was later elected as warden of Jewett City.)

New England Life

Matthew Becker was still suffering culture shock after moving nine months ago from Camden County, Georgia—where he was within walking distance from the Florida line—to Carley Avenue in Jewett City.

Matthew, twenty-nine, missed the warm weather, local eateries—even chain restaurants like the Waffle House—and the sunny disposition of people known for Southern hospitality.

In Georgia, he stood out for his passion for New England sports teams, a loyalty he developed because a relative lived in Boston. Here he blended in with the local fan base.

But he stood out on his first visit to Uncle Kranky's Cafe on Main Street. Matthew walked in with a button-up shirt, jeans, and brown slip-on shoes. "Every time I walk by there I think, 'I looked like such an idiot,'" Matthew said. "I looked like an insurance adjuster. I was a little too preppy for there." It didn't dissuade him from returning for other visits.

Matthew, who took his soon-to-be-three-year-old, Olivia, for a walk that Saturday, met his now wife, Kathleen, in Georgia. But his mother-in-law moved back to Connecticut, giving them a point-of-contact for the borough.

"We were looking for kind of a new start," said Matthew of why they decided to move to Connecticut. Kathleen was working as a banquet server at Wright's Mill Farm in Canterbury and an MRI and PET patient coordinator at Backus Hospital in Norwich.

Matthew made adjustments to life in New England. He fell in love with the seafood chowder served on Friday nights at Surrell's Pizza & Pub on Slater Avenue. It's just football and beaches where he's from, but he was getting used to basketball games at the court near the skate park on Hill Street—despite wearing sunglasses to cover up a black eye from a friendly elbow during a recent pick-up game. He was evaluating whether this was where he wanted to raise his daughter, and he was on a mission to find a job and an evangelical, nondenominational church like the one he used to go to in an area of the country known as the Bible Belt.

And that's another significant difference he has discovered here. The atmosphere among people seemed more dreary than back home, and he credited that to a lot less of God in the area.

Readers' comments;

We're not dreary, we're New Englanders. ;)

Kathleen Calvert Becker (his wife): *Thank you for putting Jewett City on the map with your book! This small town means a lot to many people here.*

A Smile Goes a Long Way

For Louis Demicco, a lifelong borough resident and longtime business and community leader, one of his greatest joys comes from the reactions people have when they receive flowers from his business.

"I like to keep people smiling," he said of the customers of Jewett City Greenhouses. "Those smiles are great."

Midmorning, Louis, sixty-six, was walking from Jewett City Savings Bank on Main Street, where he attended a monthly board of directors meeting as its chairman, to his business, where he was pitching in a little more than normal at that stage of his life because his oldest son was on vacation.

Jewett City Greenhouses entered its eightieth year on July 12, 2016. Louis's grandfather, Carmine Demicco, purchased the business in 1937 from A. A. Young, a prominent community leader whom the borough's fire department is named after. Louis said he has a photograph circa 1895 of A. A. Young riding a horse on the property, indicating at least how old the farm is. And, Louis stressed, his business is a farm—not a retail store—with an acre of glass used for the greenhouses.

Had his father, Louis Sr., not died in an accident in 1971, Louis Jr. almost certainly would have moved out of Jewett City to pursue a career in accounting. "This was my last choice," he said. But Louis joined his three uncles, Dominic, Mike and Bill, as a junior partner. The brothers had taken over the business after World War II.

It turned out to be a significant year for another reason. Louis married Jan. "She's one of the most giving persons you'll ever meet," he said. Jan was in a rush to a meeting at the Slater Library on Main Street, where she was serving as vice chairman of the board of directors.

Hard work and love of family sums up his roots, Louis said. Carmine left Italy for greener pastures in the United States, starting a new life in Jewett City. One of his two brothers went with him, establishing a business in Norwich. "You work hard, you buy property," Louis said of the two men and others like them in that generation.

Louis's two sons, Louis III and Brent, worked at the business. Louis and Jan also had five grandchildren at the time. The couple was living in a home that Louis grew up in three houses down from the business on Ashland Street.

"We've dedicated our lives to the area," he said.

Louis was proud of the borough and the town of Griswold, which he said has a great school system, several strong businesses, and political leadership that was working hard to improve the quality of life. But he worried about the borough's image, which he said was overshadowed by a drug problem.

"I used to be able to walk down Main Street and everybody knew everybody," he said of what he hopes Jewett City can return to.

Readers' comments:

You look exactly like your Dad. I remember your parents very well. The nicest folks ever.

Hi Louise you have a lovely wife. Enjoyed your story. Always loved the flowers from your greenhouse, especially the ones on my wedding day at St. Mary's. Sure has been a long time but I remember as if it were yesterday. Take care. Sandra Goncharow

Just took my mom to order her flowers for her 25th wedding vow renewal today. I wouldn't even consider taking her anywhere else.

Great story and great family. They are a giving and loving family. Always get my summer flowers from them and anytime I need flowers. The flowers are beautiful.

Where Strangers Shake Hands with Veterans

Chris Cales had been stationed at the Naval Submarine Base New London for four years. In three years from our interview, the thirty-six-year-old Washington state native could retire from the military after twenty years of service.

When he does, Chris was planning to remain here in Connecticut, after settling into a home on Barber Road in Griswold with his wife, Constance, and their three children—Daniel, twelve, and twins, Tristan and Tevan, ten.

"I'm trying to get my mom to move up here," he said. Constance was attending a nursing program at Goodwin College in Hartford, and their sons were happily settled into Griswold Public Schools, Chris said.

"It's a beautiful state," he said. "The weather is what we're used to."

Chris, a petty officer first class, has strong family ties to the military, including an uncle who served on submarines, an uncle who served in the US Army, a grandfather who served in the US Air Force, and a great-grandfather who served in the US Marines.

Chris enlisted in honor of this heritage and also with a desire to travel; he said he has seen much of the world, with special memories of Japan and Singapore. Chris has been stationed in Hawaii twice, Washington where he met his wife, and Italy.

He said he's been well received in town, where people regularly acknowledged and thanked him for his service to the country. That was in contrast to nationwide tension.

"People don't get along with one another," he said. "People are closed up with their own opinions."

Chris was dressed in his military uniform that afternoon as he picked up a prescription at Rite Aid on Main Street in Jewett City. A woman stopped to shake his hand, saying a member of her family also served in the military.

"It makes me feel good," he said. "I feel honored. They don't have to thank me."

Readers' comments:

Wow he looks like his mama. All grown up now. Thanks Chris for your service.

Very cool Chris! Congrats and enjoy that soon arriving retirement! And always, thank you for your service! Hugs

Maybe no scene captured what it means to come alive to the one square mile of your world and the hidden joys it presents than the one involving my close friends, Bob and Jaime Hamel.

Bob and Jaime weren't prepared to let all their boys back into their van for the short drive home to Central Avenue from East Main Street on the day they drove out of my friend's driveway behind me. That friend, Stephanie Hamel, and I, share a driveway.

Bob and Jaime's seven-year-old son, Micah, who moments earlier was rolling around in a puddle in the middle of a downpour with his new sneakers on, knew why.

"Because I'm soaking wet," he said, smiling.

So, under the watchful eyes of his parents who drove alongside, Micah, and his two older brothers, A. J., then twelve, and Jacob, then nine, began the trek home. His twin brother, David, drove in the van as he had a snack. He wasn't so wet.

Micah's job was to bring home a bouquet of balloons that matched his size. Bob had arranged a surprise fortieth birthday party for Jaime with a few dozen family and friends. The surprise worked—Jaime didn't catch on even after driving past the birthday balloons that had decorated the driveway. It helped that the party came a couple of weeks after her actual birthday. Micah said forty is "young."

Jaime helps lead the music ministry at the church where I am one of the ministers. She sings and plays keyboard. Bob was working as an electrical draftsman at Electric Boat's New London facility and is a retired lieutenant from the state Department of Corrections, where he worked for twenty-one years.

Micah said he had a fun time at the party. "There was a bunch of balloons, a lot of food, a lot of drinks, and a lot of things to do," he said. Those things included tag and pin-the-tail-on-the-donkey.

The walk home began with the excited discovery of a rainbow whose one end could be seen somewhere around the Jewett City Little League complex and whose other end could be seen somewhere up the road on Route 201. Micah said that meant a pot of gold was nearby. He was on the lookout.

As the three boys began to walk along the sidewalk, their clothes dripping wet, the balloons bobbing in the air, and their fingers pointing at the rainbow up ahead, Bob noted it was somehow like a scene in a movie.

Reflection and Actions Steps:
1. What are your impressions of life in a small town? What are the positives? What are the negatives? Are any values of small-town life in danger in America?
2. Start a conversation. How did the person end up in the one square mile that you both share? Based on that answer, what do you have in common other than where you live?

Janice Longton, left, and Dayle Lewis

Dakota Pedro

Bill Couture

Deb Bingell, left, and Pat Stott

Brianna Wilson, and her nephew, Brayden

Dominic Scavoni and his children (photo by Greg Hartzell)

Jo-Ann Flynn (photo by Greg Hartzell)

Tim and Leona Sharkey (photo by Greg Hartzell)

Matthew Becker and his daughter, Olivia

Louis and Jan Demicco (photo by Greg Hartzell)

Chris Cales

Micah Hamel

Rosh Disch and her children:

THE WORLD IN ONE SQUARE MILE

Al Geer (photo by Jesse Beck)

THE WORLD FOUND THROUGH THE POWER OF OBSERVATION

Lesson #8: Pause and Consider
the Unique Needs around You

A month before this project began, it felt like God led a group of us who met at a minister's living room in the borough to pause and consider the plight of a drowned Syrian toddler—Alyan Kurdi. The photo of the body of this lifeless toddler gripped and shocked—momentarily anyway—the world.

Like the prophet Jeremiah, who the Lord called to "observe" the ways of the people (6:27) to determine the true quality of life in his country, and who was led to the potter's house to reflect on the state of good and evil in nations, we were led to look closely at the refugee crisis that had engulfed Europe. We read out loud the Reuters interview of the father, Abdullah, who also lost his wife and another son, five. On the third and final attempt to reach Greece, the boat began to take in water, and when people stood in a panic it capsized. "I was holding my wife's hand. My children slipped away from my hands," he said in a police statement according to the *Hurriyet* newspaper. "Everyone was screaming in pitch darkness. I couldn't make my voice heard to my wife and kids."

It was uncomfortable, painful even, to think about. But we heard this father speak across the miles and the ocean directly to our hearts: "The things that happened to us here, in the country where we took refuge to escape war in our homeland, we want the whole world to see this."

For Jeremiah, observing and knowing the people led to prophecy and words from God that warned, challenged, and offered hope to communities across the land. That night, we saw the world is convulsing, darkness is growing, and nations are reeling. We prayed and saw once again the need for the church to wake up.

But I challenge anyone who wants to make a difference in his or her one square miles to wake up and observe the needs—to consider the needs of others. What is actually happening below the surface in your community? Who is suffering? Can you identify the top concerns? What action can you take? Far from letting the needs overwhelm and drown us in feelings of hopelessness, a closer, compassionate look will keep us from living in a bubble and inspire us to take action wherever we can—with or without the aid of formal programs. If we face what's broken, instead of just driving by day after day, some things will actually get fixed.

I offer some examples of what I observed in one year of interviews—and some small yet vital action steps that followed.

Finding Pearl

A local pastor once shared the concept of a generational curse with Autumn Matteson.

It's the idea that spiritual bondage can be passed on from one generation to another—when children inherit the consequences of the sins of the parents and the parents inherit the sins of their parents and so on—and the only power able to break the curse is Jesus.

For Autumn, twenty-three, and his girlfriend, Pearl Grimes, eighteen, it explained the misery they said they have endured since their births. That misery has included a culture of heroin, rape, abandonment, and other abuses.

Autumn and Pearl grew up separately in the Jewett City, Griswold, Voluntown area. Autumn's father, who has since died, worked for Pearl's father at one point. Autumn was on a construction job with his father when his father told him not to act up because the boss's daughter was about to show up at work. Autumn was sixteen and Pearl was twelve when they met each other for the first time.

"My jaw dropped," Autumn said of the moment Pearl stepped out of the truck. They became a couple on September 1, 2015. The date is tattooed on Autumn's finger.

"I still wake up every day and get 'I love you' and a hug," Pearl said, explaining her definition of hope.

They were living together in a tent by the Quinebaug River and spent that day looking for odd jobs to pay for food. Autumn's sneakers were falling apart; he owned two sets of clothes.

"It's a small town, and I did a lot of stupid things when I was a kid," Autumn said of why he is frequently turned down for work. "I didn't have the right guidance."

The bad behavior in his younger years included fighting, stealing, and drugs, he said. He said he recently got in a fight defending Pearl that may land him in jail. But for all the trouble he has experienced, Autumn said it makes him wonder about a better life.

"There's got to be something really big I'm supposed to do and to make me the man I'm supposed to be for the people around me," he said.

Pearl said Autumn was a hard worker. He has worked at fast food restaurants, but he wasn't able to cope yet with the pressures of public service, he said.

"People need to learn to forgive," Pearl said, referring to the constant judgment they felt they faced. "Not really forgive and forget, but I guess that's the best way to say it."

Their homeless existence led them to the back of a business downtown during the winter. "I woke up one night and by the grace of God I got her breathing again," Autumn said of one particularly cold night.

Autumn has left town a few times before. One time he and Pearl were living in New York, but Pearl's mother became really ill and she asked them to come back to be with her.

"I tried that," Autumn said of leaving the area for good. "But for some reason we just end up back here."

Pearl, who was raised by a guardian beginning at age four, offered how they plan to break the curse in their lives.

"We're not doing the bad things (our parents) did," she said.

Readers' responses:

Erika Rogers: I've lived in town for 13 years. About 19 years ago I had a friend who stayed with us for a while when we lived in Foster R. I. by the name of Amy. She was in an accident and needed a place to stay for a while. She was in love with Janis Joplin and named her daughter Pearl. I haven't seen her since she left. There is a resemblance.

There's more to this story than Erika's first response. Each time I would seek someone to profile for this project, I would pray and ask God to guide me. I had seen Autumn and Pearl downtown a couple of times prior to my interview with them. The next time I saw them sitting on the steps next to a barbershop on North Main Street, I felt to introduce myself. Autumn told me he got goose bumps when I approached them, believing it was destiny. Pearl said she felt like she knew I wouldn't judge and that they never open up like this to people. "I'm surprised we even talked," she said.

Both of them came to my house for our small group and were touched by the love they felt from the people in my living room. Autumn called me soon after that July day we met to say he needed just to talk. He was upset about a personal problem, and so I took him for a drive to Dunkin' Donuts and back. He calmed down.

A coffee. A conversation. Small, yet vital, action steps.

Regarding Erika, one of the most amazing things from this project took place between her and Pearl. In addition to the Facebook comment, she messaged me: "Hi Adam. I've been wondering what ever happened to Pearl's mom for 18 years. Pearl's mom I believe is named Amy and stayed with my husband and I for about four months when she was homeless. She left pregnant when her boyfriend came to pick her up. We were always concerned about her and the baby. I'm a teacher in the area and belong to First Congregational Church. Is there any way we could help?"

We soon learned that Amy was indeed Pearl's mom. Pearl and

Erika met at the Veterans Park and talked for more than an hour. Pearl later told me it was the first time she's ever heard nice things about her mother. It made her feel good. Erika also gave them shoes and camping supplies.

Erika was paying attention. She saw the needs. She acted.

On Oct. 14, 2016, I bumped into Pearl and Autumn at Mobile gas station on the corner of Main Street. There was an incident just earlier where they said the police harassed them. Pearl was upset and went inside the station's adjacent convenience store, Chucky's. Autumn said just when he thinks things are going well, life comes out of nowhere and hits him back. I told him about two powers. His, which is limited. And God's, which is unlimited. I asked him to say a prayer after I left. He told me he was hoping to move to Montville. And then his face lit up. "This one square mile isn't big enough for us." It's as if he wanted me to know he connected to the concept of this initiative. They did move to Montville. He called to tell me so. He sounded good.

When my wife and I reunited with them in nearby Plainfield so that I could get their permissions, Pearl reflected on the day we first met. "We were both suicidal," she said. But the timely encounter momentarily lifted them out of despair. Autumn and Pearl met Luisa and I in a parking lot outside a restaurant. As Autumn approached us, I extended my hand to his. He swatted it away and then gave me a big hug. He apologized for being late. He said Pearl was busy doing her hair and makeup in time for our visit. The next time I heard from Autumn was in an early-morning phone call on a Friday. He said he couldn't sleep that night, and every time he woke up he looked at Pearl and thought of how beautiful she was. He had considered getting a justice of peace to marry them. But then he thought of me since he knew I was a pastor. We were going to meet the next day to discuss the idea. I couldn't reach him and then weeks later I bumped into Autumn again downtown. Pearl had left him. He was due to go to jail for a few months for a fight he got in. God's not done with their story, and I need to resist the urge that every encounter I have with someone in these situations needs to end happily ever after while that person is in my life. I may never see the positive results of any good seeds God uses me to plant in someone's life. And that's okay. That doesn't change the fact that there is always hope for each of us.

High Receptivity to Friendship

Meanwhile, there was something sweet about the way two boys, one thirteen and one twelve, demonstrated their obvious friendship, finishing each other's sentences and laughing at each other's jokes during my interview with them. It's the sentences they had to finish though that saddened me.

One of the boy's grandfathers had recently died in his sleep after a long battle with lung cancer. "The first funeral I cried at was my grandfather's," he said. The boys were walking along the sidewalk across from my home on a Saturday evening on their way to play basketball at the park on Hill Street when I stopped to talk to them. The two met in fifth grade. "We were playing football at recess," one said. "And then we just became best friends," the other said.

The two friends had lived in Jewett City for three years. One moved here from New London. One moved here from Norwich; he said two days before the interview his father returned to Norwich without him. He was told it was because of bills, but he has been wondering, "Was it cause of me?" He was living with his mother, sister, then nineteen, and brother, then six. He is a Chicago Bulls fan and a Cincinnati Bengals fan.

The boy from New London said his happiest moments were when he first played football—his favorite team was the Arizona Cardinals—and when he saw his mom after she got out of jail when he was in fifth grade.

The boy from Norwich said his father is in jail for life. The two laughed about their shared fear—oceans or lakes that aren't clear enough to see the bottom. "Too much watching *Jaws*," one said. "Too much piranhas," the other said.

The former New London boy, who was living with his grandmother, said his grandfather used to make him laugh, like the time he claimed "he was the fastest man in the world. Faster than Usain Bolt." He was wearing a T-shirt with a scripture referring to John 14:6 that says, "Jesus is the way, the truth, the life." "(Jesus) is the person helping my grandfather up in heaven," he said.

I have since seen the former Norwich boy many times walking toward the basketball court just a street away from my house. I left out several details of their lives out of respect for their families. It was a painful, if not unsurprising observation—teens who live with the wonder whether it's their fault their families imploded. Too many have had a parent in jail. I don't want that to be true. But I need to know that it is indeed true and the reality for so many teens in my neighborhood. I was grateful to later learn that someone had observed the same needs and taken action.

I gave a presentation about the One Square Mile initiative at a Griswold Pride meeting later in July. Griswold Pride is a not-for-profit, antidrug program in town. Josh George, a childhood friend who is now a pastor of a church in town and a member of the organization, said he recognized both boys in my presentation because he cared for them in the town's youth recreation program. I had used the boys' story in an illustration of the need in town to reach out to our young people. I was thrilled to learn that Josh was already reaching out to them!

Josh also shared with the group an important insight: there is low receptivity to the idea that someone is trying to save someone else, but high receptivity to someone who just wants to be a friend. And friendships have to start somewhere. With an introduction. A conversation. An invitation.

A Drug Crisis

In June 2015, I was put in touch with Kevin Drobiak, a man who was in rehab in Willimantic for a drug addiction and wanted to learn more about having a relationship with God. He was a fellow Griswold High School alum. After a few attempts, we finally connected on the phone. He was soft-spoken and open to what I had to say about what it meant to find grace in God's strength. I strongly sensed his sincerity in wanting to turn his life around, and he readily accepted my offer to pick him up that Sunday for church. In fact, he told me in a text message he was looking forward to it.

When I drove up that morning, a man waiting outside the center told me Kevin was missing. He said Kevin had been kicked out for some sort of violation. The man told me he remembered how Kevin was dressed, so I asked him to get in the car with me so we could drive at least once up and down Main Street to see if we could spot him. Our search was to no avail, and I left for church so that I wouldn't be late for the service. Later that day I learned he had overdosed. My heart broke. On June 20, 2015, Darren Drobiak gave a beautiful, moving eulogy for his younger brother at St. Mary Church downtown in the borough. In honor of Kevin's favorite number—twenty-one—Darren shared this scripture from Revelation 21:4 (NIV): "He will wipe every tear from their eyes. There will be no more death' or mourning or crying or pain, for the old order of things has passed away."

Then, as I embarked on this project, never asking anyone first about the drug problem in town, I began to hear the collective stories that gave a firsthand account of how this scourge is damaging communities nationwide. People brought the subject up first. I followed with questions.

Steven Beck Jr., forty-seven, who was living on Anthony Street in Jewett City, spent time at Uncle Kranky's Cafe on Main Steet the Tuesday afternoon I met him. Steven, who worked at Ace Exterminator Co. in Norwich, told me he was troubled by the economy. "Back in the days when we had the mills going, all you had to have was one job," he said. "But now it's too expensive to live in Connecticut." Steven, who grew up in the adjacent town of Lisbon, attended Griswold High School and eventually received his GED, connected employment woes to a deep-rooted drug problem in town. "No twelve-year-old says I want to be a drug dealer when I grow up," he said. Earlier, Steven said: "I worry about the people who live here. There's been a lot of overdoses."

My favorite photo for this project was taken by Greg Hartzell, a friend who I first worked with on a documentary on my trip to Haiti. In the photo is a man towing his niece in a wagon through town. A muzzled, muscled dog stares ahead while next to Anthony Cohn. Anthony's story was another slice-of-life look at how deep the drug crisis had struck and how far its poisoned roots reached.

The twenty-seven-year-old said life for him was about family and fishing. One day he hoped to find a woman to marry and to raise a family together. For now, the self-employed contractor spent time with his niece and nephew and occasionally cared for the daughter of a family friend.

On that Tuesday afternoon, Anthony took the five-year-old daughter for a walk from his home on Slater Avenue to Veterans Memorial Park on Ashland Street and back. They were joined by a muzzled dog named Baby Girl. When another dog passed by on the opposite side of the road, Baby Girl began barking loudly and tugging at her leash. The girl, who was being pulled in a wagon, reached over and put both hands on the dog's face, telling the dog to calm down.

"She's never hurt a kid," Anthony said of Baby Girl. "She's very protective."

Three years prior to our street interview, the man had become addicted to opioids after being treated for a shoulder injury. But he had been clean and had been taking part in substance abuse treatment, he said.

He had lived in Jewett City for two and a half years when we spoke. Before that he lived in Waterford. He grew up in Jacksonville, Florida. When his sister relocated to Eastern Connecticut, he followed her because his nephew didn't have a father and he wanted to be a role model for him. That nephew was nephew.

Readers' comments:
I saw them at the park yesterday. Very nice to learn their story. I wish him the best of luck.

When I caught up with Anthony via Facebook regarding permission for this book, he offered to meet at Dean's Corner Diner downtown, where we had breakfast. The first time we talked, his reference to his addiction just happened to come up in the interview. But this time, we talked specifically about this part of his life. He said if people heard him simply say, "Don't do drugs," it wouldn't have the same impact as him saying, "This is my personal story about why you shouldn't do drugs."

His addiction began because a relative, who also had a drug problem, shared his pain medications with him. Anthony was more than happy to find relief from his year-long shoulder injury so he could get back to work and earn money. "When I started I didn't really see that the great feeling it gave me would later make me feel terrible. It's like selling your soul to the devil."

He began using the drugs at about eighteen or nineteen, and his addiction lasted about seven years. He said enough relatives had abused drugs that it seemed normal to him, altering his sense of reality. Anthony also had suffered a few personal traumatic events growing up that left him with a need for inner healing. In fact, the only time he ever cried was in church. He didn't cry anywhere or anytime else.

The breakthrough for Anthony came in large part because his grandmother, a minister, never gave up on him. Connecting with, and not condemning addicts, is proving to be vital to breaking the bond with drugs. "God was working through her," he said. His grandmother used to take him to church in Florida, and she moved back to Connecticut with the rest of the family. She served as an example of strength and love to him. "I knew there was still hope in Christ," he said. "A greater support system than just with your peers is having a relationship with God."

One definition of hope I offer is knowing something old can be made new—that whatever you are stuck in can be changed in a moment. Just like Jesus did for the disabled man who had been in the same condition for thirty-eight years. Don't give up now. Not when the lame can begin to leap with just one touch of the Savior.

When Anthony got down to the final month of his addiction, after growing fed up with his struggles, he began to reconnect with his grandmother. That renewed relationship, and the support he gave her in various conversations, led him through to victory.

Anthony's confession about opioid addiction tucked into the original Facebook story was a glance at a crisis at the side of a red wagon that had swept the nation and took root in my hometown, attracting even a visit from a US Senator who vowed federal funding in combatting the problem. Griswold Pride, led by Miranda Nagle, whose grandfather, Norman Gileau, was coincidentally the subject of another profile for the series, had been taking action in admirable ways that raised awareness and attacked the stigma associated with the crisis. The stories of real people affected by the crisis help maintain the momentum. Miranda was relentless in providing the necessary information and hosting the necessary conversations to address the battle with opioid addiction.

The Gift of Kindness

I was able to meet another man in town who, despite his own struggles, stunned me with his kindness.

I met Dennis Koncinski, fifty-nine, as he sat on the back of his truck, puffed on a cigarette, and waited for the bats to fly out of the chimney from the home across the street on Green Avenue.

The sun was setting to his left, and a breeze gently carried the smoke away from his lips as the lifelong Griswold resident said he tried to push to the back of his mind more troubling thoughts. Ten months ago, Dennis had lost his home of twenty-three years to foreclosure. The 3.2 acres were an inheritance from his father, who purchased 26 acres in town shortly after World War II. "Broke it," he said, thumping his chest, referring to the loss. "More than any woman would."

The 1974 Griswold High School graduate was unemployed. His most recent job was at Gilman Brothers Co., a foam board manufacturer in Gilman. He had hoped to retire from there, but Dennis said the company downsized three years ago and he lost his job. He also worked at Wyre Wynd Co. for twenty-eight years, starting right after high school, as a forklift operator at the former wire manufacturer in the borough. He lost that job too. Dennis was married. He said he has few friends and doesn't like to get too close to people. He also said he has been "in and out of rehab" for alcohol treatment.

At the end of the interview, I asked if I could pray for him. I consider that a powerful action step. He readily agreed.

Readers' responses:

Hang in there you are still vertical never give up.

Dennis is a really good guy. He was pretty close with my father before we lost him to cancer.

You hang in there and thank you for your service to our wonderfully free country that you served. Your community loves you

One day in October, five months after this interview, as I rounded the corner on the street where I first spotted him, Dennis drove by in his truck and waved. I stopped, reversed, and we chatted. He remembered me by name: "Adam Bowles!" And he apologized for not taking me up on my invite yet for the cell group. I called him that night and left him a message with another invite. That evening, he called back. "I called just to let you know I care." I asked him about his day. Before he hung up, he said, "Like Joyce Meyers says, I don't believe in coincidence." Joyce Meyers is a nationally known minister.

But that's not all. One day around Christmas, I got a call from Sam, my father-in-law, saying there was a gift for me from someone named Dennis. One of the cell groups I invited Dennis to was at Sam's house, so he must have thought that's where I lived. When I retrieved the gift, it was a crucifix placed neatly in a red box. Soon after I got another call from Sam. It was another gift. This time it was a mini-nativity set. This blessed me tremendously! We have since talked on the phone a few times, and we got a coffee after he returned from his time at a rehab center for veterans. He came to our cell group and then one day called me with good news: "You are one of the first to know," Dennis said. "I got a job."

A conversation. A prayer. A phone call. A gift. All actions steps.

A Leaf in the Wind

I also prayed with a man who I spotted on a summer day by the train tracks under the Route 12 bridge leading into town. I parked the truck and made my way over to him. He said he needed a moment to himself to calm down that day. He said he recently lost a carpentry job because his car that he had fixed broke down again, leaving him without transportation. That's among other problems, including suffering grand mal seizures.

The man, twenty-seven, graduated from Griswold High School in 2007. He described himself as an artist in his high school days. He didn't draw as much, but when he did it was of landscapes, particularly forests, he said. He drew the leaf that was tattooed on his forearm. In his quiet moments, he sometimes prays. "I pray for myself. I pray for my family. And I just go on another day," he said. He said he knows life gets better; he offered a definition of hope: "As long as I make it through the day, I have a couple of people smile at me, and I have a little food to eat—that's hope."

Readers' responses:
If u see this, im Praying for you.
God bless you. It will get better.

An encouraging word online from someone paying attention. More prayer. More steps. And a reminder of how important something as a smile can be to someone in need.

A Gift of Life

At her lowest point about two years ago, a twenty-year-old woman I met on Main Street thought the world was better off without her. Brittany Pope, who was living in Jewett City, lived with seven different foster families from ages three to nineteen, felt unloved and was angry at God. "I was in a dark place," she said, pausing from a walk that Tuesday afternoon from her nearby apartment just to enjoy the sunshine. "I strayed from God."

At that time, the 2013 Plainfield High School graduate was feeling a sense of accomplishment now that she was living on her own—first for a few months in Putnam and now for the last year here in the borough. She remained close to a foster respite family that she first met at age thirteen.

Recently, Brittany reestablished contact with her biological family only to discover her mother had seriously considered aborting her. Still, whereas she once thought her life had no purpose, she now said a relationship with God was the number one reason for living. She said when she was four she saw a movie about Easter at a youth group, and she decided to accept Jesus Christ into her life. She was baptized at age fourteen. She said she has lost of lot of loved ones over time, including a foster mother who died of cancer in 2006 and whom she lived with from ages three to ten.

"I know God is in control of all this," said Brittany, who was unemployed. "He is my everything. He is my world. Because of Him I've made it through." Her favorite Bible verse is Psalm 139:13 (NIV), which says, "For you created my inmost being; you knit me together in my mother's womb."

She came to one of our cell groups but later moved out of state.

I'm glad we crossed paths. And I'm glad the One Square Mile online community heard her story.

Readers' responses:

I see her walking in the afternoons when I'm picking my son up from school. She always has a smile of her face. It's nice to know her story, I wish her all the best ❤

Beautiful story! God loves you deeply!

Renee Asmar: You are an inspiration; you are very much needed by groups of people who need hope and empowerment. Any chance of speaking at youth groups or guest speaker at church related youth gatherings and ministry? Your story needs to be used, could really benefit those in need; you have walked and paid a price on a journey that is pearl of precious value. God's hand is on you; the miraculous decision of your mother NOT to abort you is a LIFE Gift of God in need of fulfillment. You have a special Mission of timely purpose. God's continued Blessings on you head to toe.

Life Is Short

As I've said, I didn't have an agenda with leading questions to steer individuals toward my preconceptions. Well, if there was any agenda it was to get people to open up as much as possible in the short time we had in the shotgun interviews. At first I applied key concepts from one of my lessons at Three Rivers in which I call on a student to stand before the class and then answer either what was the best thing that ever happened or the worse thing. That sometimes worked in this project. But the most successful question in terms of getting subjects to open up was, "When was the last time you cried?" The answer would often reveal a point of recent tension from which the person would share how they dealt with that particular hardship. Most often it was the loss of a loved one and a straightforward reminder about our shared mortality. In fact, several profiles served as reminders of the brevity of life. That alone should drive home the need for urgency in our actions.

The greatest difficulty Bill Powell ever faced was the "death of our first child. I haven't told many people about that. Fifty-one days at Yale (New Haven Hospital) was a long time. He was born with congenital heart disease. He was too small and too young to make it. It made me realize you have one shot at life—make it worth it. There's no redo. He would've been twenty-three." Powell, then fifty-two, was serving as the deputy safety officer at the A. A. Young Jr. Hose and Ladder Co, where he was working on the afternoon of October 16. "I absolutely enjoy it—keeping the guys safe, keeping the guys out of harms' way, and making sure everyone has proper gear." Powell grew up in Westbrook. "I got a job at EB years ago. I've been in Griswold sixteen years. It's quiet. It's a great little town. I've been married twenty-two years and have a twenty-two-year-old son. He's taking care of his grandmother. She's got (chronic obstructive pulmonary disease) and dementia. He's a good kid." Powell described himself as straightforward. "I tell it like it is. I don't hold back. I speak what's on my mind. A lot of people don't approve of that. It's kind of why I'm not working (as a union carpenter.)"

Readers' responses:
I love you Bill and Robyn with all my heart.

A Fight off the Battlefield

You never know the private, personal battles someone goes through. But we need to know everyone is fighting something.

As a US Army veteran who served in Afghanistan and as someone who has bounced around from town to town and state to state, Brandon Ward knew about conflict and stress.

But the twenty-six-year-old Griswold resident would rather talk about fishing, where he finds peace along local rivers, ponds, and lakes. In fact, he biked to Griswold Veterans Memorial Park the day I met him to start his first episode of a YouTube page he was calling "Fish 4 Connecticut."

"I have a passion for fishing," he said. "After I got out of the military, medically I couldn't go back to work. I want to share my passion. I met a few kids (at the park) the other day who said you should start a YouTube page."

Brandon was adopted as a teenager; he never met his birth father. He grew up in Waterford, Niantic, and Montville. His adopted parents worked nights at the local casinos and the lack of supervision for him and his two adopted brothers proved to be too much to handle for everyone, so the family moved out of state to pursue other work. Brandon lived in New Mexico, Arizona, and Florida.

He served in the military from 2008–13. "I served in Afghanistan seven-and-a-half months and was medevacked out," he said, declining further details. Brandon went through a divorce later on, even as he sought help for post-traumatic stress disorder. As many as one in five veterans who served in Iraq or Afghanistan develop post-traumatic stress disorder each year, according to the US Department of Veterans Affairs and reported by the Associated Press.

Brandon moved back to the area to visit his stepfather and stepbrother. He bought a trailer on Norman Road in Griswold. His two-year-old son, Dustin, was born missing an eye and deaf in one ear. "He's my special guy," Brandon said.

Meanwhile, he enjoyed the stress-relief fishing brought him.

"The fish are always going to be there," he said. "It's easier than people. It gets your mind off everything."

He added: "I'm putting all the pieces back together."

Brandon and his son joined us for our cell group one night. Everyone felt so blessed to have them. Dustin had such a sweet spirit. He immediately won our hearts.

Readers' responses:

Renee Asmar: God bless your healing process. I am sorry for all you endured and continue to suffer from your unspeakable tour of duty God speed. Thank God for Fishing and the healing energy that is definitely in nature.

Thank you for your service to our country. There are 100's of great fishing spots in the area. Ashland lake, Hopeville pond even the

Quinebaug river, like the other person posted, Pachaug pond, Beach pond located in Voluntown. Beach Dale pond in glasco and so many others. I grew up fishing in these places. Best of luck to you

These stories reminded me of our shared brokenness.

Matthew 10:29–31 (NIV) says: "Are not two sparrows sold for a penny? Yet not one of them will fall to the ground outside your Father's care. And even the very hairs of your head are all numbered. So don't be afraid; you are worth more than many sparrows."

God takes note of even the sparrow that falls. We also should take note of fallen lives and then see how we can pick them up, encourage them, help them. A video that went viral shows a teacher in Florida who starts each school day complimenting his students who have special needs. What a beautiful idea.

I am learning that if we go to those places in our lives and in our communities that are broken and bring them to the light, instead of putting on brave faces and masks to pretend nothing is wrong, we can begin to heal together.

Action Items and Reflection:

1. What are the biggest needs in your one square mile? How do you know this? Do you know people personally affected by these needs? How can you help them?
2. Autumn Matteson talked about the idea of a generational curse. What problems are cyclical in your community? Why do you think that is? How can those cycles be broken?
3. A pastor shared there is low receptivity to the idea that someone is trying to save someone else, but high receptivity to someone who just wants to be a friend. How would you elaborate on this insight?

Autumn Matteson and Pearl Grimes

Steven Beck, Jr. (photo by Greg Hartzell)

THE WORLD IN ONE SQUARE MILE

Anthony Cohn (photo by Greg Hartzell)

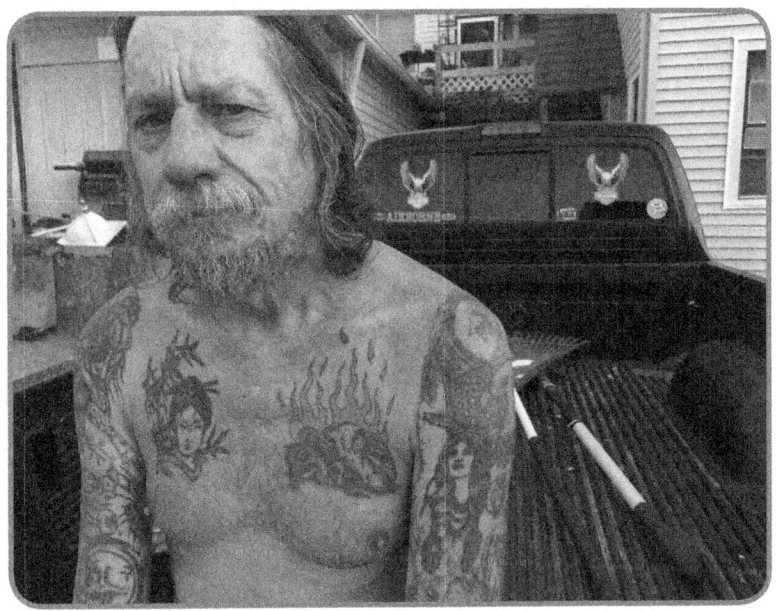

Dennis Koncinski

Brittany Pope (photo by Greg Hartzell)

Bill Powell

Brandon Ward

THE WORLD IN ONE SQUARE MILE

Lesson #9: Break Free from the Spirit and Ignorance of Isolation

We all like to think that *it* will never happen to us. That somehow the tragic events of the world won't upset our tidy, arranged, manufactured lives of peace. We know we have problems. We *all* have problems. But we won't have those problems, we tell ourselves. Not that cancer. Not that senseless act of violence. Not that family crisis. And yet, sooner or later, we come face-to-face with darkness or hardship or calamity.

As a nation, we seem to have an even greater sense of invincibility and cherished isolation. We are a land of "sea to shining sea." We have peaceful borders, even if our southern border is marked by controversial security concerns. But although we were attacked at Pearl Harbor and the World Trade Center, we took our fight with the enemy largely overseas.

Still, the world in general is becoming more interconnected. Our economies are linked closer than ever. And the speed of technology is joining—not necessarily uniting—humanity at more and more points of significant interaction. But fear of others and a false sense of superiority and security sometimes makes these interactions explosive, dangerously laced with mistrust and suspicion. On a grand scale, this fear leads to rumors of war.

The greatest outside threat in my hometown has always been the occasional hurricane and Nor'easter. But the threat that is even greater than that is internal—our own vices and weaknesses, such as heroin addiction, that causes more harm to us and our families than anything else.

We can't give into fear or retreat into hiding. It's more dangerous to think less of others.

This past year has shown me how even this tiny borough is not immune to the far-reaching events of our generation. And if Jewett City isn't, then neither is the place you live. That's not a negative statement. In fact, these events can be turned around for good, used for instructive purposes that increase our understanding and compassion of others.

In our one square miles, we can find and learn from the world. Let me explain.

On Saturday, October 1, I broke away to see if I could find a story for this project. I had just picked up my youngest daughter from soccer practice and dropped off my oldest daughter at Buttonwoods Ice Cream at a farm on the edge of town.

As I drove along Slater Avenue, I spotted two high school soccer players from the boys team. I pulled into the parking lot of Surrell's Pizza & Pub, hopped out the car, and asked them if I could do interview them right there on the sidewalk. Their English was broken, but they were happy to participate. Their brother later drove up to give them a ride, and I ended up focusing on him. This is what I found:

Carlos Sanchez kept hearing the stories of his younger brothers being harassed by gangs on the streets of his hometown in El Salvador. One of the reports included the time when William Sanchez, who was sixteen at the time of our interview, was nearly kidnapped by a gang waiting for William after school.

So Carlos urged his mother to send both William and Henry, then seventeen, to live with him in the United States. After all, Carlos faced the same dangers, fleeing the drug-fueled violence in 2009 on a trek to the US border where he eventually secured permanent residence as a refugee.

"It was a bad situation there with the gangs and the violence,"

Carlos said. "The gangs were telling (my younger brother) if you don't join us we will kill you."

In April, the brothers joined Carlos as refugees.

El Salvador, along with Honduras and Guatemala, make up what is called Central America's Northern Triangle. More than 17,000 homicides were recorded across these three nations in 2015, an 11 percent increase from the year before, according to the *Washington Post*. The surging violence triggered a wave of migrants seeking to get into the United States.

Carlos and his roommate from Mexico drove to pick up William and Henry on their walk home along Slater Avenue after a Griswold High School soccer game. Both brothers were on the team. Griswold lost to Parish Hill, 2–1. William and Henry weren't impressed with how the referees called the game.

William was in ninth grade and Henry was in eleventh grade. Henry would have graduated from high school in El Salvador the year we talked if he had stayed. They both said the school had warmly welcomed them. "It's a friendly school," Henry said.

Still, it's a difficult transition for them. Whenever they talk to their mother on the phone, she cries because of how much she misses them. "I miss my mom, my friends, my other brother, my sister," William said.

Carlos moved from El Salvador to Massachusetts when he was twenty-three. After a year, he moved to Danielson. He waited for three years before he was approved as a refugee. "You have to prove you are telling the truth," he said. Carlos said he was surrounded by people who supported him. He volunteered for *Common Borders Zine*, a bilingual, multicultural newspaper in Pittsfield, Massachusetts.

Carlos moved to North Main Street in Jewett City because he was attracted to the quiet community surroundings and the school system. He was operating his own cleaning business.

Carlos said he hoped to become a US citizen the following year, in 2017. And soon after, he hoped to sponsor his mother's residency here. He said she was not safe in El Salvador. People have been murdered in front of his home, he said.

Carlos said his faith in Jesus Christ helped him overcome his circumstances. He has a tattoo across his forearm that reads: "Inhale the future. Exhale the past."

When Carlos began talking about his life, my heart raced as I realized the magnitude of his story. He said it so casually, that he was a refugee and so were his brothers, that its impact might have been lost on me had it not been one of the subjects I read about the most.

The night before I had watched *Barbershop: The Next Cut*, and teared up—what's wrong with me these days that even an Ice Cube movie can bring me to tears—as the barbershop owner planned to move out of the Southside of Chicago because of the violence and the fact that gangs were luring his son into their violent world.

But this wasn't Hollywood for Carlos.

While Donald Trump and Hillary Clinton were fighting over whether to build a wall, and the rhetoric surrounding legal and illegal immigrants heated up to the point many times where it crossed the line into hate speech, here was a family who was here legally and represented what to many around the world see as what makes America already great. To Carlos and his brothers, we are a land of freedom and safety, a place of shelter from the drug-fueled storms that have swept their land.

To me, Carlos serves as an example of the myth of isolation.

Conflict, war, and natural disasters internally displaced a record 27.8 million people in 2015, according to a joint report by the Norwegian Refugee Council (NRC) and the Geneva-based Internal Displacement Monitoring Centre (IDMC). That's as many as the populations of New York City, London, Paris, and Cairo combined—or an average of seventy-six people displaced every day in that year. The overall total of internally displaced people around the world reached 40.8 million, including both conflicts and disasters.

And that's not just over there. That's right here. In my backyard. So many of our neighbors are having phone calls with mothers and fathers in lands where the blood of their neighbors reaches their doorsteps.

A man I met at a nearby gas station joined us for one of our cell groups. He is a refugee from Syria who said he still wakes up from dreams so vivid about his homeland that he momentarily forgets that he's here now. He said his life in Syria was in immediate danger due to his anti-government views. He used Google Earth on my iPad to show me detailed satellite images of his home. As he zoomed in, the Presidential Palace came into focus. The palace is a 10-minute drive from his home in Syria. Now he lives in my hometown.

Readers' responses to the Sanchez story:

Such nice boys! You are a welcome addition to Griswold High School!

I later learned that Henry won the top award in his class for a school wide writing assignment on the "Laws of Life." I asked him to send me a copy. He titled his essay, "New Life & New Goals." He wrote that the title reflected a "strategy to stop living in the past and start living the present in an extraordinary way, letting life surprise you day by day.

"When I decided to take my travel here my life totally changed and I knew I had to leave my past life in my old country and start living a new life here; know new people, make new friends." He continued later in the essay: "I remember on August 12, 2016 when I had to make the decision to stay or to return I had to think very well what I wanted for myself. Everything changed when I decided to stay because from that moment I released my past and now should focus on what was to come ahead."

I was inspired by the heart he showed in his writing, and it encouraged me in my own step of faith, leaving behind a familiar one square mile for others unfamiliar. In the meantime, Carlos posted on Facebook how proud he was of Henry for receiving the award. In fact, he often posts about how much he loves his brothers and how God has kept them together.

Kjell Ingebretsen's story highlights the bigger picture of how our lives intersect with world history. At the time I met him, Kjell was regularly visiting his daughter, son-in-law, and two grandchildren in Jewett City, often walking their two dogs. His own roots go overseas.

"I was born in Norway on a farm on the same bed my mother was born on. Right after World War II we had to come to (the United States) because of the devastation the Nazis did to our country. My father's job on a boat took him away for three to six months. We came to this country for a better opportunity. My father's sister in Brooklyn [New York] sponsored us," he said.

Kjell, who was retired and living in nearby Westerly, RI, recalled the trans-Atlantic voyage at age five. "I remember a little of the turbulence. We had a wicked storm. My mother was so sick. I snuck out of our room and went to the captain's quarters." Kjell likened his life's journey to today's refugees from Syria who are fleeing war and poverty.

I met this man a street away from my home. If it wasn't for World War II, it is almost certain that we would never have crossed paths. In other words, as I consider Kjell's story, the seismic impact of World War II ultimately led to a man walking the streets of my hometown. So how can I keep my head down as other events unfold around the world? Sooner or later, survivors may become neighbors. And sooner, not later, we all need to learn to get along with people of all backgrounds.

Readers' responses:

What a great idea. More towns should do this. I like human interest stories.

I saw him this afternoon walking up Ashland street. Wonderful story

I drove by my barber one evening and saw Jimmy Loarca was alone. Normally, he has lots of customers. I drove by a few minutes later and decided to visit him when I saw he was still alone. His story was another version of the American dream.

Shortly before five o'clock on this day, Jimmy was tired and nursing a sore back as he closed his barbershop on North Main Street.

But there was little time for rest even after nine hours at The Family Headquarters. Jimmy, thirty-one, was working part time as a bellhop at Mohegan Sun casino and that night's shift had him working from 6:00 p.m. to midnight.

But the labor was worth it, he said, because it was all part of supporting his family. He and his wife, Sara, had two children—Sofia, three, and Chloe, one.

"I have a lot of dreams," Jimmy said. "I want my kids to be successful. My childhood wasn't that easy."

Jimmy grew up in Guatemala, where he experienced poverty. He was four when his mother left for better economic opportunities in the United States in order to support her children. But her decision came at a cost. Jimmy was separated from his older brother, Alberto, and his younger brother, Edwin, as his two siblings moved in with family members that could only host two of the brothers. Jimmy moved in with other family members.

"I know what rock bottom is," he said. "I know what the worst is that can happen."

Jimmy used to look forward to reuniting with his brothers on Sundays, when his grandfather would take the three of them to the marketplace where the grandfather would sell watermelon slices. They then would play soccer, a sport Jimmy said he still loved.

In his spare time, Jimmy was writing his autobiography. He said he begins with telling how another member of his mother's adopted family was a forensic doctor. That doctor used to visit Jimmy, sometimes waking him up in the night, and invite him to his work. "I have another case," he would excitedly tell Jimmy. In reality, the job shadowing was an up-close account of Guatemala's violent surges as many of the cases were of homicide victims.

A year before he left for the United States, Jimmy and his brothers were reunited at another family member's house as his mother was able to pay for them to be together. When he was twelve, his mother visited to take her sons back home to the United States. It was one of the happiest days of his life, Jimmy said. "I was just so excited to have a change," he said. "I knew you could make every dream come true in the US"

His mother lived in Los Angeles and then moved to Willimantic when a friend told her there were more jobs in Connecticut. Jimmy joined her in Willimantic. Eventually, they moved to Jewett City. She was living there with Jimmy's stepdad, Jimmy's sister, and Alberto. Edwin also was living in a home in Jewett City. Jimmy was living in Canterbury, but he wanted to sell his home so he could move to Voluntown. One day, he wants to live by Beach Pond in Voluntown.

Sara was working as a dental hygienist at Goodwin Family Dentistry on East Main Street. Jimmy and Sara met during his junior year at Griswold High School at a homecoming dance. Sara was a student at the Academy of the Holy Family in Baltic but joined her sister, a Griswold student, for the dance.

Jimmy graduated from Griswold High School in 2004. Eventually, he worked at The Family Headquarters at The Slater Mill for more than two years before venturing on his own more than a year ago. He now owns the barbershop. Jimmy said he had to overcome his own fears, which often brought him to tears, and other people's doubts to become a business owner. "Nothing was going my way," he said of a particular low point a month before he opened. "I was getting angry." He sobbed. But he didn't quit. "I owed it to my family," he said. "I didn't want to let them down."

Recently, a customer asked Jimmy about his children. When Jimmy asked if the man had any children, the man said his only child died in a house fire. "I listen to people's stories," Jimmy said. "You think you have it tough and then someone else has it tougher. Your worst day is someone else's best day. It makes you realize everyone is fighting their own fights."

As Jimmy ran late that evening, his wife Facetimed him. His two girls were eating dinner before trick-or-treating. Meanwhile,

Jimmy said he was as close as ever to his two brothers. "I talk to my brothers two to three times a day."

So even the man who cuts my hair is someone whose world began far from mine. I believe that matters. I believe that's part of keeping my eyes open and being aware of something greater than me and learning to practice empathy.

Readers' responses:

Fantastic and well-written article on Jimmy. He's right, the brother's did have a challenging upbringing. But as a fellow member of his graduating class at Griswold High, we don't remember these tough challenges. We remember how you always tried, helped, and shined. Your friends all helped and happily supported you. You all instantly gelled and were superstars! I truly believe Griswold soccer is on the map because of you all. Great family and wonderful people in our community. What a kind, thoughtful, and generous person. Thanks for doing this article!

I remember vividly the day senior rule pulled me aside to let me know we would be having some new students joining us at school and how they were coming from another country. I thought it was fascinating to be able to become friends with these guys and remember our conversations not only in Spanish class, but also at lunch, in the gym around school, after practice, waiting for rides home etc. You would never know the struggles they experienced as children in another place because Jimmy, Alberto and Edwin all were such respectful positive and courageous human beings. More importantly real incredible friends. I'm so happy to hear how well they are all doing. Congrats Jimmy! Sending much love to JC!

A very inspiring story. God has a way of guiding us to our path. Never lose faith. Congratulations on your barber shop. Hope to see you, Sara and the girls soon. Love Hugs and Kisses

As beautiful as the article is, it still fails to illustrate the humble nature of this inspiring young man. Jimmy's strength is his commitment to excellence and resilience and although it is inspired by his family, it is really intrinsic. A real American Dream!

Mike Minarsky invited me to talk about this initiative on his radio station downtown called Wolverine Radio. At the end of the interview, he recommended I track down someone who works at a nearby gas station and who sang while working behind the cashier's counter. It didn't take me long to find the right person and get this story:

It had only been a month since Usman Butt had worked at Chucky's Mobil Gas Station on Main Street, but already his customers and coworkers knew how much he enjoyed singing.

That's because the Pakistani native, twenty-seven, would occasionally break into song while working at the store. The song he chose in response to my spontaneous request was about the pain of separation among two lovers after one of them leaves for a foreign land.

"He is saying don't love me because I don't know when I can come back," Usman said, after singing the song in Urdu and Hindi.

It's a song Usman could certainly relate to. He had five older brothers and one older sister. They and his father were all living in Pakistan. His mother died of breast cancer when he was fifteen. His family has tried in vain to persuade him to return home, but he insists on living here to pursue better economic opportunities. His father calls him nearly every day.

Usman moved to the United States two years prior to our talk. Before that, he had moved back home to Pakistan for a year after living and attending a college in London for three years. He was living in Willimantic when we met. He worked at a gas station in New London before taking the job in Jewett City.

Usman said he was twelve years old when he first sang in front of his father. His father enjoyed the song so much that he encouraged him to continue with music. Usman enjoyed romantic ballads and slow songs.

All this despite a hearing impairment he suffered in a motorcycle accident at age fourteen in Pakistan. He lost control of the bike on a wet road and has scars on his lip and head from the injuries. Usman sings at various parties and get-togethers.

"America is my dream," he said. "That's why I came here."

I shared his YouTube page with readers. Later, he came to our cell group at my parents-in-law's house. When the meeting was over, he sang a song in his native language for us all. It sounded so exotic, as the melodies of South Asia filled this Jewett City living room. As his family and friends liked and shared his story on Facebook, I was given an online picture of how connected we are to people from around the world. In this case, the one square mile of Jewett City was of particular interest to people across Pakistan, who lovingly and eagerly follow and support Usman's US pursuits. Their vested interest, though by degrees of separation, shows me how much more the world is becoming interconnected. In fact, Usman posted his election prediction that Hillary Clinton would win the election. He, of course, was wrong, but Usman served as a window to the American life, reporting his unfiltered opinion of life here to a circle of loved ones that rely on him for perspective. Plainly, when we treat people here with dignity, they might give a good report worldwide.

Readers' responses:

He's very polite and Sincere soul. GOD BLESS HIM

On June 4, I spotted two men by one of the town memorials on the north end of downtown. Memorials are a simple but often overlooked way for residents to learn about something bigger than themselves. We have such poor, self-serving memories. History loses its meaning. In the case of war, that can lead to taking life and our freedoms for granted. These two men showed me you don't have to wait for a formal event to honor our heroes.

This is their story:

On his motorcycle ride through Jewett City Saturday, Bill Dayon made sure he and his friend visited Fanning Park to see the memorial to those who served in the Korean conflict.

His father, Robert H. Dayon, is listed on the plaque.

The father saw combat while serving in the US Army. He was

shot in the stomach, and he also lost a testicle to injuries. "He'd wake up to those night sweats, you know," Bill said.

"He'd say to me, 'I was never supposed to have kids again,'" Bill recalled. "But here I am. That explains why I'm half nuts."

Bill, who had three grown children, was joined by Chuck Roberts, forty-eight. They became friends in high school and were both living and working in Westerly, Rhode Island, where they grew up.

"We wanted to ride through, have something to eat, grab a beer, and see my dad's memorial," Bill said. They were headed to Hank's Dairy Bar in Plainfield—the first time for Chuck. Bill worked at a lumberyard. Chuck was a property manager at an apartment complex.

Bill was extremely close to his father. Bill said his father taught him to honor the family name and to know the difference between right and wrong. Robert H. Dayon died at age sixty-two on August 31, 1994, to lung cancer.

"This means a lot to me," Bill said of the memorial. "People take this stuff for granted."

Readers' responses:

Well put Bill Dayon. first thank you for your service Robert H. Dayon 2nd he was definitely a loving family man R.I.P. and the last is you are totally crazy Bill Dayon lol

I wrote for *The Daily Campus* when I attended the University of Connecticut, graduating in 1995. In 1994, I wrote an article about this fledging technological development called the Internet. It's laughable to look back on it. It's like I was trying to describe the Internet as if it was this otherworldly entity that dropped out of the sky from aliens. I didn't grasp it, as much as I tried to write like I did. At the start of that spring semester, all UConn students had been given free access to the Internet. My lead was: "With just a few strokes on a keyboard, students can interact instantaneously with other college students and users from around the state, from around the country, and from around the world. Hong Kong,

Taiwan, England—there is no limit to travel within this world." I later quoted a student who said, "It's pretty addictive once you get to know people."

Little did we know. We are familiar with it, but the Internet remains a wonder of the world and the social media that has since developed has become an addictive, powerful way to make virtual connections to faraway places and around-the-corner places. From there, it's what we make of it. It can be used for good or evil. When used for good, it can help make a world full of strangers seem like a world full of neighbors.

You can't keep the rest of the world completely out of your world. But I love that there is so much to learn from the people around us. If you open your eyes to this reality, it just might enrich your life in surprisingly wonderful ways.

Reflection and Action Steps:

1. At a glance, how many nations are represented by your Facebook friends or other social media contacts?
2. Visit a memorial in your town. What story does it tell you about the world you live in?
3. Carlos's tattoo says "Exhale the past, Inhale the future." What does that quote mean to you? How would this quote be useful in conversation with someone you want to get to know?
4. What stories are in your one square mile that show how historical or current events outside of our nation directly affect the lives your neighbors?
5. Proverbs 27:17 (NIV) says "As iron sharpens iron, so one person sharpens another." In the context of meeting new people from all types of backgrounds, what does this verse mean to you?

Carlos Sanchez, left, and his brothers, Henry, center, and William, right

Kjell Ingebretsen

Jimmy Loarca

Usman Butt

Bill Dayon and his friend

THE WORLD WAITING AT HOME

Lesson #10: The Stories of Those Closest to You Contain the Biggest Surprises

In your discovery of the world in your one square mile, don't overlook the story of the people in your own family and in your home.

A local author, Jeff Benedict, recently collaborated with Steve Young, the former San Francisco 49ers great, to help write Steve's memoir. But the project didn't start with an idea for a book. It started with Steve's desire to share his story with his children who hadn't been born during his football days. They simply didn't know what he had gone through to achieve success.

Take the time before life passes you by to actually interview your parents or grandparents—believe it or not, they had a life before you were born! Or interview a sibling. Or a spouse.

Rick Warren, a pastor who wrote the *Purpose Driven Life*, said, "The most desired gift of love is not diamonds or roses or chocolate. It is focused attention."

Across the street from my home on East Main Street is a daycare that operates in the annex of the Second Congregational Church of Griswold.

And inside Nurturing Kids Child Care Center is a woman who pours love on every baby and child that comes into her care. She herself knows what it's like to be placed into the care of those who are not her biological parents, albeit under more dire circumstances, as she was adopted from an orphanage nestled in the mountains of Honduras.

That woman is my wife of twenty-two years, Luisa Bowles, and she's part of the inspiration for this project, *The World in One*

Square Mile. For more than a year, I enjoyed the privilege of writing profiles of the people who work, visit, or live in the borough of Jewett City. The work has been rewarding in so many ways, revealing a beautiful diversity of people that often goes undiscovered because of preconceived ideas and biases toward this community.

But I already knew the borough was a special place with special people because Luisa is in it.

In seventh grade, the year I moved to Jewett City, my mom told me the girl who was adopted by a pastor in my church was coming to our house on Ashland Street for a visit. I was immediately intrigued. When she arrived, I instinctively took her to see our parakeet. I guess I figured we may not know how to communicate to each other, but the bird could somehow prove to be common ground. She remembers that for some reason I taught her "Holy moly." I'd like to think I was far more eloquent in our first conversation.

In any case, her stories of her life in Honduras still captivate me and are one of the reasons I connect so quickly with someone from another country who has made the journey here.

Luisa's stories include the murder of her father at the restaurant he owned in Tocoa, a seaside town in Honduras. Her father was the kind of man who would give to anyone in need, including literally the shoes off his feet. When her mother feared for Luisa's safety, she took her to an orphanage in the Valle de Angeles, where Luisa spent two years and where she was teased for being "too white" compared to the other children.

She shares her childhood stories as part of the unending narrative couples tend to have; conversations that weave in and out of other conversations that write themselves on our hearts. There's so much more I could say about her life, just like I could have with each person I interviewed for this project, but one story stands out in particular. To get this story, I had to ask deliberate questions, press more than usual for details on our coffee drives. Moments like this draw us closer to each other.

In the 1980s, Nicaragua's Sandinista army fought Contras

strongholds in Honduras, displacing thousands of people from the countryside. One day Sandinista soldiers invaded the tiny town of Los Juanes where Luisa's aunt, Olivia, lived. Days before, Luisa's uncle heard about the attack and joined other men in the mountains where he died in battle. When the soldiers arrived in Luisa's village, where the homes had dirt floors, they were armed and angry, using the barrels of their guns to knock over tables. They were looking for weapons and looking for men who they feared would take up arms against them. Luisa and another aunt and other children fled for their lives from the home into the nearby forest of mango and banana trees. But they were soon surrounded by soldiers with guns drawn and aimed in their direction. Suddenly, the aunt, who was maybe four feet, ten inches tall, shouted repeatedly: "The blood of Jesus Christ has the power!" One of the leaders mocked the idea of such power. "What power?" the man replied. But miraculously the men left without anyone knowing or seeing where they went. When Luisa and the others returned to the house they expected the worse for Olivia. But she was alive and well.

Luisa, with whom I have two daughters, Tori, eighteen, and Roni, fifteen, still marvels at that day. "It makes me think that God never forgets. No matter how much in the middle of nowhere you may be—physically or spiritually—God is by your side. All you have to do is cry out to Him."

Luisa remains in contact with her mother and other family members in Honduras, but she has yet to return to her birthplace. I had the privilege of meeting her mother and visiting the orphanage while on that news assignment following Hurricane Mitch in 1998.

Readers' responses:

I have so enjoyed reading the one square mile stories- everyone had a story to tell. Luisa you are a remarkable and strong woman. ❤

Thanx for all your time posting all the info, interviews, etc. the people in our hometown & we see almost everyday in our neighborhood...;-) (y)

Beautiful

Erin Patricia: So wonderful to read these stories throughout the year. Thank you so much! What a perfect ending to the series—Luisa Bowles is such a beautiful person!!

I remember when this little girl started at GES!!! Luisa you have grown up to be a beautiful person and wonderful mom and friend to all. A great story of your struggles and accomplishments. I met your daughters at GMS lovely girls. Thank you Adam for the great stories.

Enjoyed reading about you and your wife. I lived in back of that church for some 30 years. Moved 39 years ago to Plainfield when I got married. In the years I lived in JC it was mostly Canadian French and Polish people living there. Some of my JC friends had been in the concentration camp of WW2.

Mary Lou Morrissette: *Luisa was the first person that befriended me when I move into town! I was out taking leaves in the spring that the prior homeowners had left when I bought the house in December! She graciously came over with a rake and started helping me! She didn't leave me until the job was done and I have never forgotten her graciousness! Her friendship to me and my son was unselfish! She included me in family get together and anything I needed she provided! She is an inspiration and was and is my angel! She took me to church with her when I was lost and still to this day checks in on me periodically! It's like she knows I need a smile or a friend or to remind me God is good! I love her! What an incredible journey she has had and yet she gives of herself every single day! Thank you for sharing this story!!!!*

Mary Lou's comment is a good opportunity to share her story, not because of anything dramatic, but because the joy of motherhood she shared is an example of one of the lessons I hope this book conveys—uncomplicated but powerful dreams that we all share unite us and bring out the best in a community.

At the time of the interview, Mary Lou affectionately called her nine-year-old son, Bryce, an old soul just like her.

Bryce shovels the walkway to her car in the winter without being asked, has put himself to bed since he was four, gets up early with his mom without complaint, and possesses a calm spirit mixed with a passion for sports.

"Pure joy," is how Mary Lou described him that Friday evening. "He's loving, fun, energetic. He has a work ethic for a child that I've never really seen."

Mary Lou had cried the day before because Bryce had been with his father for the week for spring break and they were missing each other, exchanging text messages.

Bryce is the reason Mary Lou left Bozrah after she divorced five years ago and settled in Jewett City. She was impressed with Griswold Public Schools; liked how the elementary, middle, and high schools are all on one campus; and was pleased with the sports programs in town. The New Jersey native knew this was the town to raise her only son.

At the same time, Mary Lou fell in love with the 1899 Queen Victorian home she discovered on East Main Street. She is the home's fourth owner. The Faust family, who the adjacent street is named after, were the original owners. But the house is commonly referred to as the Tripp home, the second owners and operators of a former lumberyard in town by the same name. It's gorgeous—one of the nicest in all of the borough.

"Everything is original, the stained glass windows, everything," she said. Bryce and Mary Lou were also joined by Brindle, a Boston terrier.

Mary Lou was working as a director of risk management at the Mohegan Tribe, where she has worked since the Mohegan Sun casino opened nearly twenty years ago.

"They've been very good to me," she said. "I can't complain. I've been able to make a life for me and Bryce."

Readers' responses:

A wonderful story in a crazy world! Bless the both of you!
So glad you chose Griswold as your home!
Awww!!! Love this! And these 2! Oops 3, sorry Brindle. ;)

In a small but meaningful way, that life has intertwined with ours. In small yet meaningful ways, our lives intertwine with others every day of our lives. Just don't forget the ones closest to us.

A Call to Action

As I close, I think back to two more moments at that conference in Atlanta.

It was quite the so-called coincidence when I bumped into Michelle Jacobik from the Norwich Worship Center at the T. F. Green Airport in Warwick, Rhode Island, just before we both had to catch separate flights to separate conferences. The pastor of her church, Jeff Sharp, is a close friend whose faith has often inspired me.

Michelle and I ended up chatting for a few minutes, and she shared how after I wrote the story on Jimmy from Guatemala, her husband visited him at the barbershop to say what an inspiration he was to him and her son. Jimmy cuts her son's hair. Jimmy is the one who usually hears other people's stories. But when I shared Jimmy's story, it opened people's eyes to his world and gave his customers a deeper look at someone whose background they had taken for granted. If I had never seen Michelle that day, I would not have known the simple yet powerful act of gratitude the story inspired.

As an encouragement to her before she gave her presentation, I gave her a page from my Bible that was already falling apart about David who attacked a city that would later be called Jerusalem. The Jebusites, who inhabited the city, first defied David and told him, "You'll never get in here!" (2 Samuel 5:6 NLT). But David, directed by God, won the battle. Often, our self-doubts and critics try to tell us the same. You'll never do it! You are not strong enough! You have failed too many times! You can't get in here! But we will overcome if we trust in God, I told her. That applies to readers of this book as well. Don't let anyone or anything talk you out of these courageous conversations, of crossing the road to get to know your neighbor, of developing the empathy necessary to help transform relationships among even strangers. Just because it isn't happening at a level that it should be doesn't mean it won't. Overcome the lies that say it won't work and the taunts that say someone else—not you—should lead those conversations. Initially this project failed to receive the necessary funding on the crowdfunding site Indiegogo. But I refused to accept the rejection as permanent.

I am so glad I pressed on by God's grace. The storytelling concept for this project, birthed in one of the poorest communities in New England, has attracted endorsement by a $300 million company traded on Wall Street. It also played a part in securing a $20,000 grant for race relations training and is the cornerstone to the equity and social justice platform of Families and Children First Griswold.

I propose that churches and school districts and community groups adopt the nearest one square miles of their area for storytelling and creative community outreach. The concept is simple. First, get to know people in your area of influence through profiles and other writing for social media. Second, use those stories and conversations to identify ways to creatively reach out to the community to address areas of concern. I believe the sharing of stories of everyday residents will develop empathy and focus on what unites us, rather than what divides us.

There is something about the concept of making a difference in one square mile— it's small enough to feel doable, conceivable, and relatable if only we would mobilize to act. The global population density, based on land area and not bodies of water, is 120 people per square mile, according to findings in "Least Densely Populated US States," by worldatlas.com, which used 2016 US Census Bureau estimates.

But slowing down to take interest in other people can happen in even dense areas.

Jewett City and the City of London may be separated by the Atlantic Ocean, but they have something in common—both areas are roughly one square mile. On a recent trip to London, I made it my mission to visit the western entrance to the original area of London known as the Square Mile. Several businesses proudly refer to themselves by this nickname. The population sizes in both places are obviously much different, but the lessons learned through *The World in One Square Mile* apply whether in a small town or a big city. My family and I only had time on our walk along the Thames River to step just past the monument marking the western entrance. As I finish my Jewett City journey, I feel like I'm standing on the edge of a bigger world with new discoveries and new people to meet.

The second moment at the Atlanta conference is about a woman in a wheelchair whose first name was Jenny. She immediately struck up a loud conversation with me, holding up people in line for breakfast. I waved them by. "What do you hope to learn?" she asked me in a way that startled me. "Why are you here?" I told her briefly about One Square Mile, and she immediately offered advice. "Don't say poor them, or poor that. Write about their gifts." It will create empathy, she said. That advice stuck with me. Don't spend too much time on what people can't do. Focus on what they can do.

What is empathy?

I can think of no better definition than one actually lived out by one of my youngest daughter's friends, Aaloki Patel. When Aaloki first arrived to Jewett City from India a year before, my daughter and her friends in middle school at the time were kind enough to include her in their Christmas gift exchange. The girl, now a teenager, has not always found it easy to adjust to life in America, struggling with English among other things. The next Christmas, the group of friends changed slightly and the teenager from India was somehow overlooked. But Aaloki remembered their kindness and bought them gifts. I shared at the beginning of this book that my family and I were preparing to move overseas. The thought of this goodbye was hard on all of us, but particularly my youngest daughter, Roni. Just the mention of our move often brought her to tears. So you can understand why we all felt emotional when Tori, who told us the story on behalf of Roni, showed us the card Aaloki got for Roni.

"Wish you a Happy Holiday and Merry Christmas. Thank you for being my friend. I know how you feel, when we move to another country, but I gone miss you!"

I know how you feel. There's power in that kind of understanding, which is much greater than a shallow sympathy.

I later visited her and her family to ask her what she thought of creating a card that we could distribute to new immigrant students in Griswold, along with information that would help welcome them to the community. I included this proposal as part of a second phase, outreach project for *The World in One Square Mile* that received a grant from Families and Community First Griswold. The original card she made included the word *welcome* in several different languages on the cover. On the inside it said, "Welcome to Jewett City." And on the facing page she wrote, "Hello, welcome to Jewett City. We know that it's hard for you to move in different country. And you meet different people, different language, and maybe you don't know that language, but you still come to that country, and live there. That's really good. And you be kind with everyone. That's really nice of you. We hope you like here, and we hope you feel same here as you fell in your own country. Thank you for coming."

The card will be edited, but it blesses me to think this is one small result of this initiative.

Tori said when she thinks of Aaloki, a glimpse she had of her one day stands out in her mind. It's of Roni's friend, dressed in an Indian sari, dancing in the rain in her driveway.

Meanwhile, the Wall Street company that later hired me to write stories of its customers is CubeSmart, based in Malvern, PA. When our family was down to one vehicle, I would drive my oldest daughter along Route 138 to and from Buttonwoods Ice Cream stand, which took place as often as several times a week during the summer. On these drives, I would pass by one of CubeSmart's storage facility, featuring rows of nondescript units in a rural, open area. I originally considered approaching the company to see if it would be interested in joining our list of local sponsors who helped fund a portion of the project. In fact, if it wasn't for the initial support of United Community and Family Services, a health center in Norwich that had an office in Jewett City and was planning to build a much larger facility in town, I don't know how far I would have gone. The center gave $1,000, which encouraged me that people in general would support the project. Altogether, I received $2,750 from fourteen businesses. Obviously, that's not enough to make a living. But I believed that eventually the initiative would grow in spectacular ways.

In the end, I decided not to ask CubeSmart for a contribution like the other local businesses. For some reason, I felt there was a bigger opportunity. I had no idea that this storage facility was actually just one of eight hundred nationwide for a company with one million customers. Or that the company was blogging about the communities it served. Once again, I saw a bigger picture to the so-called small world I lived in. That's part of what faith is all about! After weeks of waiting, I finally had a phone call with two of CubeSmart's media directors. Immediately, they connected to the proposal, understanding its potential and the power of story as it relates to their business. In a matter of minutes, we had one of the most emotional conversations of the past year—again with strangers. One of the two women took special note of one of my questions I routinely ask people: "When was the last time you cried?" She voluntarily shared the last time she cried was that morning. She had been in a rush and late to work, feeling the stress of life in general, when she watched as nineteen geese crossed the road. There was something about the sight of these carefree animals that made her laugh. And then the laughing turned to tears as she was forced to pause and reflect on a scene that brought her peace.

Then she asked me when was the last time I cried.

It was the first and only time all year that someone turned the question back to me. It was a vulnerable moment I wasn't prepared for—just like all the other moments I had written about. Like Norman Gileau, the retired principal, who wiped away tears talking about his wife who was in a nursing home. Like the teenager with the guitar strapped to her back, who wiped away tearstains before she let me take her photo. Like Dayle Lewis, who wiped away tears while talking about the love her mother once shared with her father, who died years earlier. Like Sorel Sylvain, who wiped away tears sharing the miraculous turnaround from drug addict to street preacher.

So I shared my story. I didn't know if it was the last time I cried, but it was the most memorable. My wife and I had been concerned about our oldest daughter, whose faith was being tested through various circumstances, including the idea we would be moving overseas. She had just graduated high school, and her friends had scattered to different colleges while she felt her own life slipped into limbo. At the same time, Luisa and I felt incredible emotional pressure that comes along with such a move. One day, after dropping Tori off at work, Luisa asked if I wanted to hear something. Earlier, Luisa had been on the second floor of our home when she heard Tori playing the keyboard and sweetly singing the words to "Oceans" by Hillsong, a massively popular Christian band from Australia. Her bedroom door was closed, so Tori wasn't playing to impress anyone. It was clear this was her prayer. The lyrics include:

Spirit lead me where my trust is without borders

Let me walk upon the waters

Wherever You would call me

Take me deeper than my feet could ever wander

And my faith will be made stronger

In the presence of my Savior

Luisa decided to record Tori without her knowing. We later let her know and got her permission to share this story. As soon as I heard Tori declaring her trust in God, I was reminded that everything would be all right, that God is in control, and that He cares about me and my family more than I'll ever know. Luisa didn't notice at first, but the reassurance brought me to tears as I was driving. I would have sobbed had I not been behind the wheel.

What a year it was. Random strangers became friends, or friends of friends, such as Alisha. Alisha, by the way, the one who I rushed outside to meet while still in my socks, took me up on my invite that same day to attend a dinner at my friend Stephanie Hamel's house right behind mine. Stephanie, her sister, Megen, and Alisha became friends. In the summer, Luisa and I joined them on a hike. Alisha and my daughter, Roni, share the same birthday. On January 17, Megen posted to Alisha's Facebook wall: "Happy Birthday! Hope you have a wonderful day! So thankful that we've met! Thankful for that sidewalk! Ha!"

Alisha responded with a heart emoji.

That sidewalk, or what that sidewalk represents, has led me to many people I am thankful for.

Dakota, Rebecca, Usman, Autumn, Pearl, John, Alisha, Brandon, Johnny, Dennis and Brittany all attended our cell groups. I met a professional trick pool player, talked with lifelong friends in the middle of their walks, heard stories of budding romances, and listened to people who in tears shared how much they missed loved ones.

I talked with a man whose wife of forty years died the night before due to complications with pneumonia and muscular dystrophy and who was reminiscing with his two neighbors on the porch of their apartment even as I approached him.

When the borough held its first Annual Downtown JC Bike Night, held in honor of T. J. Sumner, a Jewett City firefighter who died unexpectedly the year before at the age of thirty-one, I talked to two bouncers who mingled with the hundreds of bikers who attended the special event. One of them, nicknamed Moose, pulled out his phone to show a video of his family's pet deer. Yes, pet deer. Bucky, which he had raised since a friend found the fawn on the side of the road after its mother had been killed by a driver, would "come in the house, watch TV, play with the kids." But, it too, was killed by another doe.

In short, walls began to come down. People began to open up.

I found truth to this admonition in James 1:19 (NIV): "My dear brothers and sisters, take note of this: Everyone should be quick to listen, slow to speak and slow to become angry."

Yes, be quick to listen. You don't always have to be the most interesting person in the room. Let someone else be.

What I found were dreams as big as the world that transcend our boundaries and its nearly 3,500 residents. People battle fears, depression, and loss. People raise their families, seek for love, and hope for a better tomorrow. We are one square mile of husbands and wives, dads and moms, sons and daughters. We are one square mile of heartache and healing lived out in homes, banks, baseball fields, skateboard parks, pizza parlors, pharmacies, and backyards. I've met World War II veterans, cancer survivors, world travelers, business leaders, and many more here. We are one square mile, but we are America and we are the world. Take my advice—go and discover this world in your own one square mile. After this one-year adventure, I can now practically guarantee the one square mile you live in is far more interesting and wonderful than you may take for granted.

Mary Lou Morrissette with her son, Bryce, and their dog, Brindle (photo by Greg Hartzell)

Adam and Luisa Bowles

CPSIA information can be obtained
at www.ICGtesting.com
Printed in the USA
BVOW03*0734020917
493797BV00001B/1/P